Fundamentals of Aviation Crisis and Emergency Management

This book takes the topic of aviation crisis and emergency management and walks the reader through what aviation organisations must consider alongside legislation to respond fully to an aviation emergency or accident. It offers both theory and practical tips and ideas along with templates and checklists to help build confidence in how to run an aviation emergency operation. This includes timelines for activation, setting up and managing humanitarian centres and how a full aviation crisis operation runs at the site of the accident.

Fundamentals of Aviation Crisis and Emergency Management is the only textbook available with all required elements laid out chronologically. The reader can plan for, train for, and exercise for a multitude of crisis examples, building both confidence and competence in managing an aviation emergency. *Fundamentals of Aviation Crisis and Emergency Management* includes a range of case studies and a variety of interviews with those people who have experienced an aviation crisis and deployed to it. This allows the reader to fully immerse themselves in the topic and makes the book both a textbook of key knowledge and also a book that can be read for increasing understanding of the topic. It will be essential for aviation students and professionals, disaster response organisations, and emergency planners.

Gail A. Rowntree is Associate Professor in the School of Aviation and Security at Buckinghamshire New University in the UK. As former cabin crew and then a responder for both Kenyon International Emergency Services and Go Crisis, Gail has written several articles and chapters on trauma, resilience and response to aviation disasters, having deployed in a variety of roles to over 40 international incidents.

Aviation Fundamentals
Series Editor
Suzanne K. Kearns

Aviation Fundamentals is a series of air transport textbooks that incorporate instructional design principles to present content in a manner that is engaging to the learner, at an accessible level for young adults, allowing for practical application of the content to real-world problems via cases, reflection questions and examples. Each textbook will be supported by a companion website of supplementary materials and a test bank. The series is designed to help facilitate the recruitment and education of the next generation of aviation professionals (NGAP), a task which has been named a 'Global Priority' by the ICAO Assembly. It will also support education for new air transport sectors that are expected to rapidly evolve in future years, such as commercial space and the civil use of remotely piloted aircraft. The objective of *Aviation Fundamentals* is to become the leading source of textbooks for the variety of subject areas that make up aviation college/university degree programmes, evolving in parallel with these curricula.

Fundamentals of Airline Operations
Gert Meijer

Fundamentals of International Aviation
Suzanne K. Kearns

Fundamentals of Airline Marketing
Scott Ambrose and Blaise Waguespack

Fundamentals of Statistics for Aviation Research
Michael A. Gallo, Brooke E. Wheeler and Isaac M. Silver

Fundamentals of Airport Planning
Theory and Practice
Ravi Lakshmanan

Fundamentals of Sustainable Aviation
Eva Maleviti

Fundamentals of Aviation Crisis and Emergency Management
Gail A. Rowntree

For more information about this series, please visit: www.routledge.com/Aviation-Fundamentals/book-series/AVFUND

Fundamentals of Aviation Crisis and Emergency Management

Gail A. Rowntree

LONDON AND NEW YORK

Designed cover image: © Bjoern Wylezich

First published 2024
by Routledge
4 Park Square, Milton Park, Abingdon, Oxon OX14 4RN

and by Routledge
605 Third Avenue, New York, NY 10158

Routledge is an imprint of the Taylor & Francis Group, an informa business

British Library Cataloguing-in-Publication Data
A catalogue record for this book is available from the British Library

ISBN: 978-1-032-52121-3 (hbk)
ISBN: 978-1-032-52118-3 (pbk)
ISBN: 978-1-003-40533-7 (ebk)

DOI: 10.4324/9781003405337

Typeset in Times New Roman
by Apex CoVantage, LLC

This book is dedicated to my family, be they human or canine. To all the people I have served during deployments, to those I have worked with as a responder, to my students who continue to inspire me, to those people who gave their time to help me with their reflections and experiences and not least, Robert, for your patience whilst I was writing this book.

Contents

Case Studies

Figures

Tables

Introduction to the Book

Welcome to the Fundamentals of Aviation Crisis and Emergency Management. This book is aimed at aviation personnel whose job it is to plan for an aviation crisis and respond to it on behalf of their airline and managers who will need to lead their teams through one. For certain roles within an airline, it's not 'if', it's 'when' a crisis will occur. Not always high-profile media events with tragically large numbers of deaths, but more likely aviation crises that still require experience, expertise and training.

To date, I have attended over 40 incidents for several disaster management organisations with Kenyon International Emergency Services[1] and Go Crisis.[2] This book does not claim to take away any of the knowledge and expertise these organisations have, but as aviation grows and rebuilds in a post-pandemic world, I felt it was time to put pen to paper (on a laptop) and share both my experiences and those of the people it has been my privilege to deploy with. Any of the deployments I discuss were always at the request of one or other of these organisations. They gave me experiences that I am forever grateful for and gave me the opportunity to meet some wonderful and giving humans. This book is partly dedicated to those organisations, the people I have met and the people with whom I have deployed.

Introduction

This book is designed to support both the personnel working in aviation whose role it is to plan for disasters, work to ensure a plan is trained and exercised and ultimately manage a crisis or emergency, should the need occur. It is also to offer students in aviation and aviation emergency response a detailed understanding of the key teams and areas of a disaster operation. Also, a timeline for when the key decisions or actions should be taken. Finally, the book is designed to help those in the industry have a better understanding of what happens in areas that they might never work.

The book balances theory and practical situations – the reality with the lived experience. There are elements of this book, such as checklists, templates and suggestions, to help the reader prepare for a response. This means that airlines can use them to help pre-response to be ready for such events. An example is the crisis communications statement templates in Chapter 8, when external communication is required in a tight timeline in the early stages of a response. Another example is the kit lists for Go Team members or Special Assistance Team members to prepare for deployment.

The book also includes interviews with those who have attended some of the worst disasters in recent aviation history. How did the theory meet with reality? What lessons did they learn? How would they do this differently? These can be read on their own and form a sincere and earnest picture of the lives of those who choose to deploy to aviation incidents.

DOI: 10.4324/9781003405337-1

There are sections called *'tips'* that include ideas and helpful hints to consider when planning, training, exercising or even activating staff for a crisis. Also, there are sections where personal experiences, called *'observations'*, have been included. These may be small things to consider when responding to accidents or observations around themes that have emerged during deployments.

The book is split up into two logical sections, starting with how the current legislation from ICAO Annex 13 (2013)[3] came into effect: *'we need to know where we came from to fully understand why we do what we do'* (Annex 13).

The first chapter will explore the current legislation and regulations concerning aviation accidents and disasters, who the key agencies and authorities are that interact and cooperate throughout a response to enable a swift process of identification of the deceased, and support for the survivors and the families of everyone impacted.

Chapter 2 will then move into understanding what an aviation response plan is and how best to recruit volunteers or responders in a world of Netflix®[4] where disasters look exciting, there is never any blood and the bodies are always in one piece. It is about how to balance reality whilst managing the expectations of responders and what support, training and exercising volunteer responders need to be fully ready to activate for any aviation crisis.

Chapter 3 centres on Crisis Management Centres (CMC) and their role in aviation accidents. The CMC is a physical location, but since the pandemic of 2020, these have also been successfully run remotely. The roles of those who work in the CMC remain the same, whether physical or not, and are crucial for its success. The chapter will also review the required resources and what equipment it needs to run efficiently. The answer simply is – not as much as crisis managers might think.

The chapter includes how the CMC works closely with call centres or, as we will refer to it in this book, a 'TEC' or Telephone Enquiry Centre. The term TEC and call centre can be interchangeable along with contact centres as it also includes the written communication that society is so used to now through emails, SMS and social media platforms. TECs collate and disseminate vital information, and data is shared with both the CMC and the authorities managing the accident itself.

Finally, in chapter 3, a timeline will offer a clear overview of how a disaster should be run from initial activation through handing over management of the operation to the team at the scene. The CMC also features in Chapter 11 when closing down the operation.

Go teams are, in aviation terms, the small teams of specially trained personnel who initially deploy to a scene of an accident to assess and review the resources, equipment and reality of what they witness *'on the ground'* back to those being asked to make high-pressure decisions, usually in the CMC. Chapter 4 explores in detail the role that Go Teams have in arriving to support those airline staff who have been *'holding the fort'* since the start of the crisis, either at the departure airport, arrival airport or an airport in between if an accident takes place there. Go Teams also set up initial services and infrastructure for the other teams following afterwards, i.e., Special Assistance Teams (SATs).

The chapter includes a handy 'kit list' for those managing Go Teams and a case study from an experienced Go Team member on what it feels like to be the first to deploy and what they have learned from this role. This chapter offers a glimpse into the world of activation and deployment by sharing some insight into how it feels to walk into the hornet's nest of a high-profile disaster whilst being easily identifiable as belonging to the organisation that may (or may not) have killed many individuals. This role takes a special kind of individual, and choosing them is vital for the success of early media coverage and family and friends' perception of how the airline is treating them.

Finally, Chapter 4 reviews the communication and working relationships between the Go Team, CMC and third-party agencies, i.e., NGOs and investigation authorities, from embassies who support their own nationals and families through to local suppliers for flowers or candles at memorials. Each has a unique role to play and they are often overlooked in planning. The role of NGOs and charities in a new, more global disaster world is vital to advocate for families and survivors of aviation accidents, and how these parties all interlink, communicate and work together for the good of everyone involved is key to success.

Chapter 5 goes on to explore the role of a SAT member, a volunteer internal airline staff member who deploys to accidents to support survivors and families of the deceased. The chapter reviews the types of actions and tasks that a SAT member might be expected to undertake each day and also evaluates some of the challenges and problems they can face whilst at the Humanitarian Assistance Centre (HAC) (covered in Chapter 7). Due to operational requirements and resource issues, many airlines reinforce their SAT numbers by using external SAT experts utilised from Third Party Providers (TPP). Airlines often have contracts with TPPs to 'retain' the expertise of professional SATs who supplement the numbers and help to run the HACs for their clients.

Often, SATs will support families in their own homes, and the chapter explores how the support differs from that at the HAC and some of the obstacles that can arise.

Alongside the airline response is a well-planned airport response and, in Chapter 6, the book describes the differences that an airport has to consider in its plans and how they support survivors and families and friends meeting a flight if the accident occurs on the airport land. The chapter also looks at the regulations and legislation that surround airport response to an airline accident and the various rooms and equipment needed to ensure a safe and secure environment until the transfer over to the HAC or onward travel, depending on the size and nature of the crisis being managed.

Once transferred over to the HAC, Chapter 7 takes a look at how to set one up and run an operation from there for the survivors, the families and, potentially, teams and agencies working together at the accident site. How the CMC transfers management oversight and decision-making to the 'Incident Management Centre' (IMC) based (usually) at the HAC and all of the services and support offered for those staying there. This is where the SATs may be based in supporting families who choose to travel to the HAC or survivors who have chosen to come to the HAC to gain further information and details from the authorities and agencies working from the site and investigating how the accident took place.

Setting up, running and managing a HAC sometimes feels like setting up and managing a small city. The chapter takes the reader through the key actions and also how reality can sometimes skew the best intentions. It will answer questions such as: where to locate a HAC? Who has access to it? What does the organisation have to pay for? For how long? And what happens at a centre? The chapter will include field experiences in the form of a case study by an experienced SAT Responder who has worked in several HACs and who understands how theory, legal responsibility and reality can sometimes build into a high-pressure environment. Understanding the lines of responsibility when working with families is helpful to minimise mistakes.

A core element of modern disaster management is crisis communication and the associated media interest these events bring with them. Chapter 8 takes a detailed dive into the world of crisis communications and offers the reader templates to support both statements and social media injects but also how to work with the media, in its many forms, to give and receive vital information to help the authorities investigating the incident and the survivors and families involved. The chapter will evaluate the importance of giving statements within a tight timeline regulated by the legislation of ICAO Annex 13 and the Family Assistance Act (1996/2000). It goes further to include what's expected of those who face the cameras and give a press conference. What to include in written communication to families?

Often, organisations find themselves trying to balance the support for those impacted along with protecting a brand and share price. This can and often does lead to conflict and criticism. Chapter 8 dissects the challenges and offers solutions to them. One such example is whether or not to include a 'dark site', often maligned, and, with organisations desire for transparency, it can lead to problems and issues of hacking, malicious actions by individuals or contradictory information.

Chapter 9 offers an introduction to understanding grief and also explores some of the most common religious and cultural 'norms' around this topic. This is especially useful for SATs who have to work with families and survivors at the HACs. How do religious and cultural requirements after the death of a loved one balance with the identification and investigation process? This is often a potential conflict area, and because grieving is such an individual journey, navigating this as a responder can be challenging.

Working in line with the centre are other areas of the operation that might not be so central to the operation as they are often managed and controlled by outside parties. Chapter 10 offers an insight into how these groups work and link to the HACs and families staying there. The work of outside groups relies heavily on expertise but also being able to build positive working relationships with the organisation, Go Teams and SATs, as well as those managing the HAC. Elements such as search and recovery at the crash site itself. Teams that work on finding, processing, cleaning and returning personal effects to families. Forensic teams that work to offer families a positive identification of their loved ones and support families in making decisions about key areas, including repatriation. Giving families the power to make the decisions they think are best for their loved one. Finally, Chapter 10 includes a case study by an experienced search and recovery professional about the importance and significance of the work they do for aviation crisis and emergency management.

Chapter 11 brings the reader to the point of closing an operation and starting to unwind the processes, procedures and working arrangements that can be in place for several months. It revisits Chapter 3 on CMCs and activation and shows how to reverse the process so that the first group of people who opened the HAC are the last set of people to close it. How management, decision-making, and data are securely dealt with and passed back to the organisation to support the ongoing investigation. It will also consider the sensitive issue of closing a centre and sending families home, who may have been there for several weeks and may not have a positive identification of their loved ones. How SATs can communicate the closure in a way that does not add more trauma to the families. Handing over support to a team based at the organisation and how communication and information will be offered post closure.

Sending home Go Teams and SATs from a high-pressure and emotional arena can be a potential challenge for organisations. The chapter offers some suggestions and recommendations for SAT and Go Team wellbeing and post-accident support. To enable them to transition back into the workplace without long-term distress and trauma is vital. It is also an area that is often missed, so this chapter guides those whose job it is to manage these volunteers in how to successfully help them back to their lives and jobs. Reviewing the accident response by all parties involved and making changes to the process form part of this continuous feedback loop from those who were there and those who experienced it.

Finally, Chapter 11 looks beyond the accident at memorials. Part of the requirements of the Family Assistance Act (1996/2000) is often lost in the accident response itself and post-accident review. Planning for a memorial takes time and effort and will include both an event and a physical memorial. The chapter concludes the cycle, taking the reader up to the one-year anniversary of the event itself and the key considerations needed for what is always a high-profile event in the media. However, it must also be something the families feel part of and have decision-making power over. This can raise challenges, especially where cultural, religious or geopolitics form part of the mix.

Definition of Key Terms

In aviation, there is a wide range of different terminology and phrases used interchangeably for what are, in essence, the same thing. To ensure clarity for the reader, the book will use the following terminology.

For any crisis or emergency, it's best to use one phrase. Certainly, the range of crises and emergencies that can happen to an airline are vast, but this book concentrates on the far end of the scale. That is, where death or injury has taken place and requires a full response operation. For that end, the term 'accident' will be used as it links directly with the International Civil Aviation Organization's (ICAO) definition.

ICAO uses the term 'accident' to determine emergencies that require a full plan activation and responding to it by personnel.

Annex 13 defines an accident as

> An occurrence associated with the operation of an aircraft which, in the case of a manned aircraft, takes place between the time any person boards the aircraft with the intention of flight until such time as all such persons have disembarked, or in the case of an unmanned aircraft, takes place between the time the aircraft is ready to move with the purpose of flight until such time as it comes to rest at the end of the flight and the primary propulsion system is shut down, in which: a) a person is fatally or seriously injured as a result of: – being in the aircraft, or – direct contact with any part of the aircraft, including parts which have become detached from the aircraft, or – direct exposure to jet blast
>
> (ICAO, 2021, p. 13).

There are critics of the word *'accident'* (Easthope, 2022), and this is acknowledged as a challenging term to use where often the resulting reports suggest it was not an accident at all and, of course, there is a myriad of other terms that could have been chosen in its place, such as *'incident'* or *'disaster'*, but on balance, using the clear definition from ICAO seems to be the least problematic for what is a complex and sensitive area of research.

As such, this book will also refer to those who have lost their lives in an 'accident' as 'deceased'. Most forensic agencies and aviation authorities will use the term 'human remains', i.e., INTERPOL and ICAO, and, on occasions when referring to a forensic process, that term will be used, but this is not a book that covers the forensic processes in detail. A top-level introduction to 'Disaster Victim Identification' or DVI is offered in Chapter 10 but only as a means for the reader to understand the whole operation and, therefore, how this process fits in with the support offered at the HAC or from a CMC.

The HAC is a safe and secure physical location set aside for the injured and families of the deceased to come and receive direct information and updates from the various agencies and authorities, to talk to the authorities and ask questions and to offer their own personal information in the form of DNA to support a positive identification of their loved one.

This term is used interchangeably with Family Assistance Centre or FAC. For the purposes of this book, they mean exactly the same thing. Preference is given to HAC as it has an international understanding but some of the references used will refer to the FAC as well. ICAO defines this as *'the provision of services and information to address the concerns and the needs of the aircraft accident victims and their families'* (ICAO, 2013).

Finally, the term *'airline'* is preferred to the ICAO use of *'air operator'*. This has been chosen purely for simplification, but the definition is the same: *'A person, organization or enterprise engaged in or offering to engage in aircraft operations'* (ICAO, 2013).

Additional Inputs to Support Understanding

Each chapter includes learning objectives so that the reader can see what they can expect to learn from it. There is an opening quiz to test what the reader might already understand.

 This means there is a tip that offers the reader a useful additional point to consider.

 Where this icon is used, there is a personal observation from the author's field experience that offers context or added perspective for the reader to consider.

The chapters all include individual glossaries at the beginning because there are so many aviation acronyms, and if the reader is not confident with them, they are readily available, so the reader does not need to go back to the beginning of the book for clarity.

Some chapters include case studies or examples to add specific detail, and some chapters include interviews with field experts to share their experiences.

At the end of each chapter, there are questions, scenarios or case studies for the reader to consider, ensuring they have understood the content.

Notes

1 Kenyon International Emergency Services, a US- and UK-owned disaster management organisation.
2 Go Crisis, a UK owned disaster management organisation.
3 ICAO Annex 13 – Aircraft Accident and Incident Investigation.
4 Netflix® is a subscription TV organisation.

References and Additional Reading

Easthope, L. (2022). *When the Dust Settles. Stories of Love, Loss and Hope from an Expert in Disaster*. London: Hodder and Stoughton.
Family Assistance Act. (1996/2000). (Online). Available at: www.ntsb.gov/tda/er/Pages/tda-fa-aviation.aspx.
ICAO. (2013). *Assistance to Aircraft Accident Victims and Families, Doc 9998/499*. Montreal: International Civil Aviation Organization.
ICAO. (2021). *Annex 13 to the Convention on International Civil Aviation Organization: 12th Ed. Aircraft Accident and Incident Investigation*. Montreal: International Civil Aviation Organization.

Part I

Legislation, Regulation, Key Agencies and Organisations Involved

1 Understanding the Legislation and Key Agencies Involved in Aviation Accidents

Chapter Objectives

By the end of this chapter, you will be able to:

- Understand and explain the key legislation relevant to aviation crises and emergencies
- Describe why it is important to have a good working knowledge of the key legislation and where to find it
- Explain what a family association is and their involvement in aviation accidents
- Describe the relevance of the Montreal Convention for families at the Humanitarian Assistance Centre
- Demonstrate your understanding of the key concepts by completing the quiz and exercise at the end of the chapter

Opening Quiz

1. What does ICAO stand for, and where are they located? What is their main responsibility?
2. What is the Montreal Convention?
3. What is the Chicago Convention? When was it initially created, and how many freedoms of the air are there?
4. What is the Family Assistance Act (1996/2000)? Why was it created?
5. What is a family association? What role do they play in supporting aviation crises?

Glossary for this Chapter

CAA   Civil Aviation Authority
DVI   Disaster Victim Identification
HAC   Humanitarian Assistance Centre
ICAO International Civil Aviation Organization
SAT   Special Assistance Team
TPP   Third Party Provider

DOI: 10.4324/9781003405337-3

Chapter Introduction

Aviation is a global industry with a combined income worth $838b in 2022, with an annual increase rate of around 5% from 2009 to 2019 (Statistica.com). It employs hundreds of thousands of people and carries millions of passengers. It is an industry that is legislated and regulated with an emphasis on safety, but still accidents occasionally occur.

Globally, in 2022, there were five fatal air crashes with loss of life involved. That is from a total of 32.2 million flights in 2022 (IATA, 2022). That means a passenger would need to fly every day for 25 years (statistically) to be involved in an accident. The industry works hard to ensure the odds are minimised, and this book offers an inside view of how airlines and authorities work together to achieve a seamless response for each accident that occurs. Figure 1.1 illustrates the global map of aviation accidents by region and associated numbers according to ICAO.

Aviation Legislation

Aviation disasters and family assistance are legislated so that airlines and airports can plan and work towards a consistent goal of response and service for those who will need to use it at the time of an accident. The core of all the legislation is how to respond to any airline crisis or emergency on a scale of magnitude so that those involved, such as survivors and families of those deceased or impacted, are taken care of.

The main legislative areas were originally derived from the Chicago Convention[1] signed in 1944 by 52 signatories and have since been added to now measuring over 150 signatories.

The Chicago Convention is the basis for most of today's legislation and regulations in aviation, and although the freedoms of the air that the original document are rooted in around the rules of operation, it is worth exploring the most relevant for aviation crisis and emergency management as they sometimes form a challenge to responding especially if overseas from the airline home base.

The Chicago Convention was signed towards the end of World War 2 in 1944 and was meant to structure the regulations around aviation in a post-war world. So called because it was signed in Chicago, it offers the nine 'freedoms of the air'[2] that aviation still follows today.

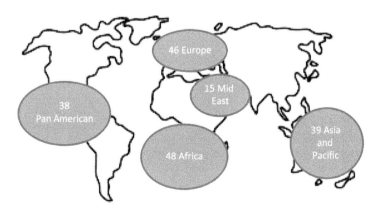

Figure 1.1 Map of global aviation accidents by region

Adapted from ICAO (2021b) Safety Report

The '*Freedoms*' lay out how commercial airlines can operate their schedules, but each State can, on occasion, decide to apply a change to the '*Freedom*' depending on the circumstances. Aviation disasters would allow for this.

The Freedoms of the Air Relevant for Aviation Disaster Management

There are nine 'Freedoms', and a full description of each can be found on the ICAO website. Five were the 'original' agreements from the Chicago Convention, with another four added afterwards. All would potentially be a possibility for an aviation disaster, but the key 'freedoms' for an aviation disaster would be:

An airline from State One is being given permission to land in State Two for refuelling (non-traffic purposes). (**Second Freedom**) This could include a 'Go Flight' or a special flight carrying families or media, etc.

Carrying passengers and putting down from State One (home carrier) into a foreign destination (**Third Freedom**). Again, this could include a 'Go Flight' or a specifically agreed non-scheduled flight for families.

Carrying passengers from State One, picking up passengers in State Two and carrying them onto State Three for a final destination (**Fifth Freedom**). This might be an unscheduled pickup of responders or families '*en route*' to a final destination on one flight.

Carrying passengers between two 'foreign States', i.e., State Two and State Three, when the original state is State One (**Seventh Freedom**).

Adapted from ICAO Doc 9626 (2018).[3]

The Chicago Convention also led to the creation of the International Civil Aviation Organization known as ICAO.[4] This is now the leading body that regulates legislation for aviation. The main annexes and documents relevant to the subject will be referred to throughout the rest of the book.

Airline Responsibility

Keep in mind that although several agencies are involved in an aviation crisis and emergency operation, the airline is ultimately accountable for the support offered to families and survivors. The airline can partner with many outside businesses to support them in terms of Special Assistance Team members (SATs) and Telephone Enquiry Centres (TEC); the airline can work with airports, hotels and partners and exercise together, share plans and resources.

Although the book goes into detail about all of the elements of airline responsibility throughout the chapters as they arise, it is worth noting that Third Party Providers (TPPs) may be asked to be responsible for key elements or a response such as managing a Humanitarian Assistance Centres (HAC), but throughout the response, the airline remains accountable to the authorities and as such must be mindful of how much delegation is appropriate for each element of the operation.

The airline is responsible for releasing an accurate passenger manifest to the designated State office or department within the defined time period and then undertaking the management and operation of an HAC for the survivors and families of those impacted.

The airline must have adequate numbers of trained personnel to undertake support for those involved either at the HAC, hospital or in their own homes and must also offer a toll-free telephone number or contact centre for those who think they may have loved ones involved to receive initial information.

The airline must provide transport to and from the HAC along with reasonable living expenses whilst there for survivors or families who wish to travel. The airline must coordinate access to the various agencies that can offer information and answer the survivors' and families' questions whilst at the HAC on areas such as the progress of an investigation, the process of positive identification for the deceased and offer access to the initial findings before being released to the media.

Under the Montreal Convention,[5] the airline is responsible for an early payment for financial assistance to families and survivors, although this is often undertaken by their insurer. This is to ensure short-term bills can be paid without causing undue distress.

The airline should provide counselling or psychological support both during the response operation and also afterwards that may fall outside the initial agencies used, i.e., Red Cross.[6] An example might be that a survivor needs long-term psychological support for the trauma they suffered as a result of the accident, and the airline would be responsible for the provision of this service.

The airline is responsible for the return of the deceased to their families and potentially the funeral arrangements as well, but this is in liaison with families at the time as funeral arrangements may be covered by individual insurance policies taken out at the time of travel.

Finally, the airline is responsible for the recovery, potential repair and cleaning of personal effects to the families and survivors and the longer-term storage of those items not initially claimed.

Any memorial services and sites for memorials themselves would also fall under the responsibility of the airline.

Finally, the airline is responsible for the longer-term support of those impacted by their accident, and this could include financial support, emotional and psychological support or other legal requirements that might befall the survivors or families of the deceased.

Airlines should have all of these responsibilities planned for, trained for, exercised, provisions made available and understand what the extent of the airline's long-term involvement is with those who have been impacted by the accident.

Key Regulations and Documents Relevant to Aviation Accidents

ICAO Doc 9998 (2013b) – Policy on Assistance to Aircraft Accident Victims and their Families

This document identifies who is responsible for supporting those people involved in an aviation accident. The core of the document is an explanation that '*family assistance is the provision of services and information to address the concerns and the needs of the aircraft accident victims and their families*' (1.1, p. 11). Who should come to the (HAC)? How is the HAC run? Why is it necessary? Where should it be located?

The requirement for detailed support for those involved is that it may need national legislation to ensure each 'State' can accommodate the specific needs of those who may need post-accident support and ensure that what is offered is enough for the response it may be accommodating. For clarity, each sovereign country is referred to as a 'State' and not a regional area, as in the US.

The airline responsible needs to ensure that the financial and personal needs are taken care of for anyone involved and that the providers of family assistance (airlines and airports) have the funds to undertake such an operation at short notice.

Usually, the cost of family assistance is taken care of by insurance policies the airlines need to have in place in order to gain a license to fly, but still there is a potential gap between the beginning of a response operation and the insurance policy initiating. Airlines need to start the process of activation and deployment by having funds in place to start with to pay for early expenses, i.e., transportation and/or accommodation for Go Teams, etc.

Airline plans need to have a comprehensive understanding of who will be supported at the HAC. Not necessarily by defining exactly who should be supported but by what types of assistance might be offered. Further, the airline plans should explain when family assistance should be activated and detail how TPPs will be used if they are part of the plan, as well as when and where. These airline emergency plans must be tested periodically and, nationally, the legislation can be more rigid in one State than others, but a general rule is once every year for testing the plans through an exercise of some significant level.

Any policies within the airline that pertain to the country's legislation should be included. There may be specific legislation that might be singular to a country or several countries. An example is EU996, which is specific to the European Union.[7] All emergency plans should be audited periodically for their continued appropriateness, their effectiveness and whether there are elements that are still required or need changing, i.e., the change of TPP or contacts within the airline due to a change of role, etc. Any audit can be undertaken internally but definitely externally.

Moving on, Doc 9998 asks airlines to define how the plans are enacted once activated and who or what agency coordinates and manages the operation; anything that requires legislation or, at the very least, regulations on how the agencies involved will communicate, share data and information and work together at the HAC. This includes how the airports should establish immediate support and have robust plans that are consistent with the airlines and the legislation. Airports must also exercise their own emergency plans and have them periodically audited as well. Airlines and their local airports are required to work together in terms of exercising and training to facilitate seamless family assistance as required during a real accident.

Emergency plans for airlines will largely be based on where they are located. The Family Assistance Act (1996/2000)[8] is US in original but adopted largely around the world and gives a more practical explanation of what should be included in an HAC, additions and alterations according to the type and size of accident and the resources required, both equipment and personnel. Adoption of the Family Assistance Act across different countries can mitigate against some of the issues that culture, specific individual State legislation and regulations can bring.

ICAO Doc 9998 helpfully offers the main providers of support to families in the event of an activation of the airline emergency plans. These are:

1. The Government of the State of Occurrence (where the incident happened) and other States who are involved in the operation. This then requires that at a State level (national level), cooperation is key to successful assistance.
2. The airline itself, who holds **ultimate responsibility** for any assistance operation regardless of who undertakes it on their behalf.
3. The relevant airport if required. An example might be for families waiting for a flight at a destination that will not arrive.
4. TPPs and, finally, Family Associations (if required). TPPs are non-governmental commercial businesses that partner with airlines and airports to supplement the resources and sometimes the equipment required for a full response. They are paid a retainer for these services. In the US, this might also include aid agencies such as the Red Cross, who can take the role of Special Assistance Team members or other services such as logistics and accommodation, etc.

(Adapted from ICAO Doc 9998, 2013b)

Doc 9998 also clearly lays out the commitment needed by the airline with regards to support, communication and basic needs:

- Information about the occurrence to authorities, those involved, their families and wider society
- Emergency response to the accident; how the airline responds in the short, medium and long term
- Coordination of travel to, and lodging at, a HAC as well as assistance to those not travelling. Not everyone travels to the HAC, but they are still entitled to be supported by the airline
- Coordination of a visit to the accident site, where access is practicable
- Support for immediate financial needs through the Montreal Convention
- Information about the location and status of the victims and the recovery, identification and disposition of human remains before communications are given to the media
- Information regarding the recovery, management and return of personal effects
- Social, emotional and psychological support; and
- Information about the progress of the investigation and its objective

(Adapted from ICAO Doc 9998, 2013b)

ICAO Doc 7773 – Manual on Assistance to Aircraft Accident Victims and their Families[9]

This manual lays out in detail the how of assisting families and survivors of aviation accident.

It offers definitions of the key terms needed for each party and agency that may be required for an incident. This includes a definition of 'family' and 'accident' in Chapter 1.

Chapter 2 of the manual takes a more detailed look at what family assistance should look like and what assistance must be considered in plans. This includes how information is shared and what information the families at a HAC (or at home) should be party to. This generally is around notification of positive identification of loved ones, key stages of the investigation, etc. Also, how the response at the crash site is progressing. The focus of informing families is always that they must hear about any progress or news before the media or social media platforms can share it. This can be a challenge given the speed of communication, but it should be the guiding rule for informing families.

Another communication that the document outlines is sharing the progress of personal effects recovery and management. This access to information is through the daily briefings at the HAC.

If applicable and appropriate, then a visit to the crash site for the families forms part of the assistance laid out in the document. This is not always possible due to the location and geopolitical challenges that may surround the crash site, but if access is allowed and safe, then this should be considered part of the communication and assistance offered to families at the HAC.

Immediate financial needs must be met at the HAC. This can be in the form of expenses for accommodation and lodging but, more widely, the payment given to families at the Centre under the Montreal Convention.

Montreal Convention 1999

The Montreal Convention (1999) was formerly known as the Unification of Certain Rules for International Carriage by Air Doc 9740 and originally known as the Warsaw Convention.[10] The Convention also covers baggage damage, loss and delays in normal operational circumstances or domestic travel, but for this book, the focus will be on its purpose for the bodily injury and death of a named passenger. Note that it covers passengers on board the aircraft but does not cover third-party non-passengers on the ground who may be caught up in a disaster. Originally, it was entered into by 152 signatory States of a possible 191 (De Gama, 2017).

The Convention sets out the minimum standards required by airlines for payment to the next of kin. This initial payment, called the Standard Drawing Rights (SDR),[11] is a *'hardship payment'* that is for the relief of immediate expenses that must be paid within two weeks of the accident. In Art. 28, the Convention explains that the airline should ensure prompt payment of the SDR and *'make advance payment without delay'* (Montreal Convention, 1999, 28:10).

Advanced to both survivors and the next of kin of the deceased, it is paid by the insurance company contracted by the airline as this is their responsibility as part of the Family Assistance Act (1996/2000) and in no way admits liability by the airline (De Gama, 2017). Article 21 of the Montreal Convention was revised in 2019 to an upper limit of '128,831' made up of any named currency (usually local) or a mixture of currencies as each case deems appropriate. It is often paid at the HAC directly to the individual identified as the legal recipient. It is non-returnable except in specific cases that are outlined in Article 20 (Brown, Efthymiou & McMullan, 2022). It is worth highlighting that the sum paid is deducted from any final compensation agreement.

Finally, the document lays out that families should be offered *'social, emotional and psychological'* support (ICAO Doc 9973, 2013a, 2.1:19). Who should be supported and how they may need support is, of course, unique to that family.

It can be a challenge to know what each family needs, and the document acknowledges this in Chapter 2, as there can be cultural, religious, national and demographic differences that mean each family may need something completely different. The core of the legislation is that support should be deemed 'fair', and this includes how many members of the family come to the HAC, how that group is made up and how long they stay. This is hard to plan for and really needs to be determined at the time of the accident. The basics of what might be deemed 'best practice' support can be agreed by training by TPPs who have vast experience in these areas and understanding previous experiences by 'Family Associations'.

ICAO Doc Annex 9 (2016) – Security and Facilitation. Border Controls and Procedures[12]

ICAO Doc Annex 9 is really centred on the facilitation of operations. Chapter 10 will introduce this. It is concerned with the repatriation of human remains and assistance to families after an accident takes place. It also details the challenges and responsibilities around border controls and documents for transporting human remains.

 Tip

Read each of the key documents associated with aviation crisis and emergency management. They can easily be downloaded from the websites of ICAO, NTSB and State CAA. Make sure you are familiar with them and understand where you need to go for specific information on a response phase, action, responsibility or communication flow.

Highlight the key areas that are fundamental to response, plans, training and exercises so you know where to find the exact detail you need if you are in a hurry.

Keep the documents up to date with the latest version in case regulations or legislation changes, and you might find it helpful to print them off and keep hard copies for future reference.

ICAO Annex 13 (2021a) – Aircraft Accident and Investigation

Annex 13 is centred on the process required after an accident has taken place. This includes who needs to be informed, in what order and with what information

It goes on to define injuries, death, investigating authorities and other key areas such as State of Occurrence (see 'Key Terms' for more detail).

The main purpose of Annex 13 is for airlines and those involved in aviation crisis and emergency response to understand the roles and responsibilities of all those involved.

The document refers to each of the key agencies and authorities involved in an accident and these are offered in more detail in what follows.

ICAO – Annex 13 – Key Agencies Involved in an Aviation Disaster

Although ultimately the airline is responsible for the management and operation of an accident, they do not work in isolation, and there are many other groups, organisations, departments and agencies that are involved as required by the legislation and regulations detailed earlier.

Investigating Authority

This is usually authorised by the State of Occurrence unless that State does not have the skills, infrastructure or resources to be able to undertake this role. In this instance, they can ask for help or even delegate it to another country under ICAO Doc Annex 13. This means a different State will take over the investigation in support of the State of Occurrence and work collaboratively with them to ensure a successful investigation.

The State of Registry will also take over the investigation if the accident takes place outside the borders of any State, such as international waters. Occasionally, the State of Registry may take over the investigation if the accident happens within a State that is not a *'contracting State'* to the legislation or regulations. Essentially, the investigation will be led by the State that the parties agree to.

As defined previously, the State of Registry, Operator, Design and Manufacturer will all be represented in the investigation to enable the collation and dissemination of information by each party. Each party will also support the Investigating Authority in any activities they are asked to that enhance the investigation or add to evidence or data. An example might be the State of Manufacture handing over all documentation and logbooks for the aircraft concerned. Representatives of these States will also travel to the crash site to support investigation teams on the ground.

The role of the Investigating Authority is to investigate an accident and, according to ICAO Doc Annex 13 (3:1), *'not to apportion blame'*. This is for the subsequent inquiry and proceedings through courts to determine.

All States involved in an aviation accident have a responsibility to support the various agencies called upon to manage the accident but especially the investigation authority as Figure 1.2 details.

States that have Passengers onboard the Aircraft

All States that have passengers as citizens that survive or are deceased will send representatives or support those citizens either to travel to the HAC, communication challenges, i.e., languages, financial support, representation at the HAC, completion of documentation for visas and repatriation, etc. Often, this will take place at the local embassies or similar but can take place at the

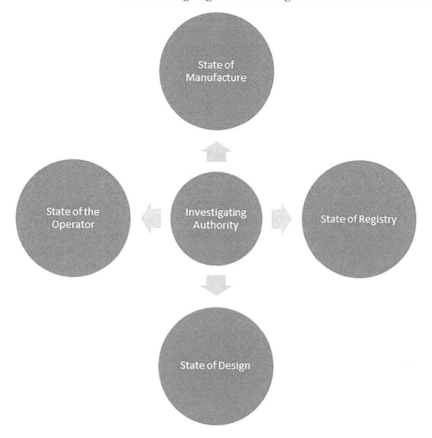

Figure 1.2 How the States support the investigating authority

HAC, depending on the numbers involved. The representatives for each State will work closely with the Foreign Office or State Office to ensure everyone impacted by the accident is offered the appropriate support they are entitled to in their time of need.

State Foreign Office

The Foreign Office for each State should be in possession of the passenger manifest with the agreed timescales as per ICAO Doc 9973 (5:18). This is discussed in detail later on but links back to the Chicago Convention and the various freedoms in that they are responsible for ensuring families and survivors can enter or leave the State of Occurrence as quickly and smoothly as possible whilst not circumventing the rules of entry. An example of the complexity of undertaking this was around the aftermath of 9/11 when hundreds of aircraft had to land in non-scheduled locations without necessarily the '*right to land*', either for the aircraft or for the passengers.

The State Foreign Office would need to ensure anyone '*landing*' would be in possession of an appropriate (temporary) visa to do so. The State Foreign Office would work closely with Customs and Immigration to expedite any visas required for families to attend specially set-up HACs. This key element was added to ICAO Doc Annex 9 (2016) via a resolution in 2001 (A32–7) to ensure '*facilitation to enable expeditious entry into the State in which the accident occurred of family members of the victims of an accident*' (p. 3).

The State Foreign Office can support translation services again through embassies or through official Governmental organisations. They may also expedite the correct documentation, official stamps and customs permission required to repatriate the deceased or medically evacuate the injured as requested. Again, quickly and smoothly but without contravening any of the set freedoms or rules in place.

Case Study 1 – Adaption of Immigration Rules during 9/11

During the 9/11 terror attacks, many aircrafts were diverted and had to land in locations that were not part of their scheduled flight plan. This involved passengers who had *'landed'* in the US or Canada (for example) but did not possess the correct documentation and visas. As the international Governments did not know how long the diversions would last, the various State Foreign Office departments worked hard to ensure all passengers impacted could get off the aircraft, if necessary, for overnight accommodation with a temporary visa. Once they were allowed to continue their journeys, the passengers could leave the *'State'* and go to their final destination. ICAO Doc Annex 9 allowed for this provision for aircraft accidents and, along with the Chicago Convention, meant passengers impacted could be housed safely without being left on the aircraft. Under ICAO Doc Annex 9, *'The State of Occurrence of an aircraft accident and adjacent States shall make arrangements to facilitate the entry into their territory on a temporary basis of family members of victims of an aircraft accident' (8.41)*.

Civil Aviation Authority

This is a domestic authority, so each State will have its own Civil Aviation Authority (CAA) that upholds the regulations for aviation within the State. They certify both aircraft and license crew to fly them. The CAA will regulate safety and security within airports and for airlines within their areas. They are responsible for the aviation industry within their jurisdiction. This includes family assistance both at airports and at a HAC. Not for managing or running them but for having oversight of any plans, training and auditing those plans to make sure they are suitable and workable, if needed. Often, the CAA will undertake or observe multi-agency exercises to ensure collaboration and communication between agencies that fall under their authority.

Post-accident, the CAA will review their safety and security provisions and may deem it appropriate to bring in new policies and procedures, if required. An example might be a new procedure for baggage searches within airports after a security incident or terror attack.

International Civil Aviation Organization (ICAO)

Set up post the Chicago Convention, the International Civil Aviation Organization is a Montreal-based regulatory body that ensures aviation is kept safe for all passengers by ensuring a set of regulations and legislation are agreed upon by all 'signatories' that adhere to the regulations to enable them to fly commercially. Each State is represented with a tri-yearly meeting and more regular '*assembly meetings*'. There are several layers of decision-making with the regulatory body that gives each State a way of being 'heard' and being part of the body. Most of the regulations are in the form of 'annexes' that take a specific topic to detail the requirements that States and commercial airlines follow.

Coordinating Agency

ICAO Doc 9998 asks that on top of the agencies working hard collaboratively during an aviation accident, and there should be one agency that facilitates and coordinates the operations and communications and ensures *'proper relationships'* between all parties.

Each State will have to name this coordinating agency within their national and local plans. It could be a named person or a group that brings together the various agencies to work together, to communicate with each other, to have an overview of what each agency is doing and to ensure the operation, assistance, and support works for the *'victims and their families'* (ICAO Doc 9998, 2013c, 2.3:6). They may organise and open the family briefings at the HAC (family briefings are covered in more detail in Chapter 7) or organise agency meetings to share information. It is a facilitation role but an important one to make sure the operation, which can be vast and complicated, is kept on time, covers everything that is required for a full and detailed investigation and ultimately so that the families and survivors have the answers they need and the support they are entitled to during the operation.

Responders

Responders can be local or national level emergency responders and include police authorities, the military, medical responders and search and rescue agencies. Essentially, these are all personnel who have a role in the rescue and treatment of those involved in an aviation accident.

Other roles as a responder could involve securing the site, rescuing those who may need triage and transferring to hospitals and helping with the initial accounting for those who may have survived and where they have been transferred to, i.e., the hospital or a hotel or airport. This book does not go into detail about the roles and responsibilities of these parties apart from acknowledging their importance in any initial rescue, security and control of accident sites.

Third Party Providers (TPPs)

As stated, airlines often work with expert outsourced organisations that they contract to help them in areas such as supplementing their trained personnel to support families and survivors, search and recovery, personal effects, repatriation and other related services. Although the TPPs may be able to take a lot of the initial strain away from an airline and provide expertise that the airline may not be able to provide, the airline remains responsible for the provision of any of the services contracted out and must keep a keen eye on the management of the providers to ensure a high level of service and quality. Figure 1.3 shows that the airline must balance the responsibility they have for supporting families with bringing in the experience and expertise of a TPP.

Airport Operator

Along with the airline, one of the main parties that can be involved in an aviation accident is the airport operator. In ICAO Doc 9998, it states that they should also have *'plans and provisions in place to provide assistance . . . . For the immediate care and support following an accident'* (2:20).

This may involve the airport of departure, arrival, both or one that is closest to the accident itself. This might be a connecting airport that many of the passengers involved came through either as a party or to catch a specific flight to a final destination.

The airports must provide a secure and safe area for survivors who may be transferred to them for temporary aid. Alternatively, it could be to support those families who have dropped

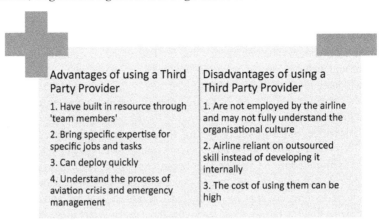

Advantages of using a Third Party Provider	Disadvantages of using a Third Party Provider
1. Have built in resource through 'team members'	1. Are not employed by the airline and may not fully understand the organisational culture
2. Bring specific expertise for specific jobs and tasks	2. Airline reliant on outsourced skill instead of developing it internally
3. Can deploy quickly	3. The cost of using them can be high
4. Understand the process of aviation crisis and emergency management	

Figure 1.3 Advantages and disadvantages of using a third party provider

off loved ones on departure or are waiting for them at the arrival airport. The areas need to be secure, safe and away from the media. Chapter 6 goes into the details of these areas.

Family Associations

ICAO Doc 9998 clearly defines Family Associations. These are groups of *'interested people'* (2.5) who have been impacted by previous accidents and come together to form associations. They can advise at a State level for legislation, support airlines and airports for standards, offer guest lectures, provide training and sit as advisory board members.

Family Associations form such an integral part of understanding how it feels to receive the support from a response that ICAO has included them in their policies and especially in Doc 9998. ICAO recognises them as an organised group and not just an ad hoc group of volunteers. They bring with them a very personal perspective about how it feels to be the service user for the whole process of assistance. Many airlines use them as guest lectures or for training for their volunteer staff and seek their guidance for improvement of emergency plans, etc., post-accident. Based mainly in the US, these Family Associations are growing, and their involvement to improve the whole process can be invaluable. Table 1.1 offers an overview of the key agencies who would be involved in an airline accident and all of the parties and agencies they could potentially interact with.

Conclusions

It is vital that anyone working in the aviation disaster industry in any role must have a working knowledge of the regulations and legislation pertinent to them. Not necessarily in deep detail, but know what each document is based around and where to find the right information to answer questions.

This chapter gives an overview of those key agencies and parties that the rest of the book will explore in much more detail. The key 'players' in an aviation disaster and their role in it.

Each party has a clearly defined role, and using thorough and well thought through and exercised plans, each party knows what they have to do if required, what they need to provide, what equipment and resources they may need and what personnel with particular skills and expertise are needed to undertake an operation.

Table 1.1 Overview of the key agencies and parties involved in an aviation response

Agency or Provider	Key Responsibilities	Works with
Investigating Agency	Overall investigation of the accident itself Produces the interim and final report	State of occurrence (if different or delegated) State of registry State of manufacture State of design Coordinating agency Governments Airline Airport (if involved) Associated family members and survivors Third Party Providers Family associations Media DVI teams Responders
Coordinating Agency	To facilitate the key agencies and parties to work together, communicate and produce a coordinated investigation and operation for the survivors and families of the deceased	State of occurrence (if different or delegated) State of registry State of manufacture State of design Investigation agency Governments Airline Airport (if involved) Associated family members and survivors Third Party Providers Family associations DVI teams Responders
State Foreign Office	Offers embassy or consular support for survivors and families as part of a national Governmental response	Airline Airport Associated family members and survivors Governments Customs and Immigration Embassies and Consulates
CAA	Ensures Family Assistance provision is within their regulations and jurisdiction and reviews safety and security policies and procedures post-operation	State of occurrence (if different or delegated) State of registry State of manufacture State of design Coordinating agency Governments Airline Airport (if involved) Associated family members and survivors Third Party Providers Family Associations
Airline	Responsible for the overall response of the operation and the support of survivors and families	State of occurrence (if different or delegated) State of registry State of manufacture State of design

(*Continued*)

Table 1.1 (Continued)

Agency or Provider	Key Responsibilities	Works with
		Coordinating agency
		Governments
		Airline
		Airport (if involved)
		Associated family members and survivors
		Third Party Providers
		Family associations
		Media
		Employees of airline
Airport	Responsible for the initial support of survivors and families	Coordinating agency
		Governments
		CAA
		State Foreign Office
		Airline
		Third Party Providers
		Family associations
		Media
		Families and friends
		Survivors
		Other passengers
		Other airlines (i.e. alliance partners)
Third Party Providers	May have a role as part of a contracted service agreement with an airline	Airline they contracted with
		Investigation agency
		Coordinating agency
		Governments
		Embassies and consulates
		DVI teams
		Responders
		Associated family members and survivors
		Salvage teams (to remove wreckage)
Family Associations	Offer guidance and advice pre-operation and post-operation	Airlines
		Governments
		CAA
		Associated families and survivors

From international bodies such as ICAO through to government-led agencies and commercial and aid agencies, each group knows what they must do, how they must work together for the benefit of all those involved and when they are required as part of a coordinated response to an aviation accident.

Key Points from this Chapter

1. ICAO covers the legislation surrounding the responsibilities of the various parties when a response occurs
2. Each department or agency has a clear role to play and a clear process for areas such as communication
3. The airline has clear responsibilities within the ICAO legislation and the Family Assistance Act (1996/2000)
4. All parties involved in the manufacture through to the registration of an aircraft have a clear line of responsibility but can also delegate responsibility to other parties if unable to enact their roles

Quiz

Take a few minutes to complete this quiz to check your understanding of this chapter.

1. Name the key Annexes from ICAO that link directly with aviation crisis and emergency management.
2. If required, the State Foreign Office should ensure the quick and smooth expedition of visas for travelling families, but not at the expense of what?
3. List three areas that the airline is responsible for as required by the Family Assistance Act.
4. Who do airlines sometimes work with to delegate expertise, services and resources in a disaster? Are airlines still responsible overall if they have delegated any service elsewhere?
5. What is the Montreal Convention, and what is the hardship payment that falls under the Convention called?
6. What is a Family Association? How do they support airlines to have a better understanding of their responsibilities during an accident?
7. When was ICAO founded, and what is its main role in aviation?
8. What role does a 'Coordinating Agency' take during a disaster operation?

Exercise

Take a look at the short overview of ABC Airlines in what follows and consider the following:

Where is the 'State of occurrence?'
Where is the 'State of design and manufacture?'

Overview of ABC Airlines

ABC Airlines is a Hungarian-owned and based low-cost airline flying mainly in Europe with some routes in North Africa. They fly Boeing 737–800s. ABC123 (registration Z-PLKC1) departs from Budapest at 2200 (local), enroute to Luton (UK). They crash just outside Paris in fields at approx. 2345 local time. There is currently no indication of survivors.

Notes

1 Chicago Convention – Original documented agreement (1944) of international cooperation and regulation for aviation.
2 Freedoms of the Air – The original regulation contained within the Chicago Convention that set down the rules of flying between nation states.
3 Freedoms of the air adapted from Manual on the Regulation of International Air Transport (Doc 9626, Part 4).
4 ICAO – International Civil Aviation Organization. Based in Montreal, Canada.
5 Montreal Convention (1999) Document that sits with the International Air Transport Association (IATA) that pertains to the airline responsibility for passengers in the case of delays, lost baggage etc. but also covers injury and loss of life.
6 Red Cross – International Committee of the Red Cross. Established in 1863, they are a worldwide organisation that supports people caught up in war, conflict, famine and disease and also supports victims and families of aircraft disasters.

7 EU996 – A European-wide policy on the investigation and prevention of air accidents and incidents in civil aviation.
8 Family Assistance Act – Subcommittee on Aviation of the Committee on Transportation and Infrastructure, House of Representatives, One Hundred Fourth Congress, Second session, 5 September 1996.
9 ICAO Doc 7773 Manual on Assistance to Aircraft Accident Victims and their Families.
10 Warsaw Convention – Forerunner for the Montreal Convention (1999). Sets out the obligations for civil aviation that cover delays, lost baggage, injury and loss of life for passengers.
11 Standard Drawing Rights (SDR) – from the Montreal Convention that states the initial payment to survivors and families who have lost a loved one. A no-blame payment that is agreed internationally to support hardship for those caught up in a disaster. See Montreal Convention.
12 ICAO Annex 9 – Policy on Security and Facilitation. Border Controls and Procedures. This document is essential for the transportation of human remains across borders and details the process and documentation required.

References and Additional Reading

Brown, L., Efthymiou, M., & McMullan, M. (2022). Recovering from a Major Aviation Disaster: The Airlines' Family Assistance Centre. *Sustainability*, 14 (7). https://doi.org/10.3390/su14074040.
De Gama, R. (2017). *The Exclusion of Liability for Emotional Harm to Passengers in the Warsaw and Montréal Convention: Moving Away from Floyd, Siddhu and Pienaar to the Stott Case?* http://dx.doi.org/10.17159/1727–3781/2017/v20i0a827.
Family Assistance Act. (1996/2000). (Online). Available at: www.ntsb.gov/tda/er/Pages/tda-fa-aviation.aspx.
IATA. (2022). *Annual Safety Report. Executive Summary: 59th Ed*. The original copy of this document can be found at: https://www.iata.org/contentassets/a8e49941e8824a058fee3f5ae0c005d9/safety-report-executive-and-safety-overview.pdf.
ICAO. (1944). *Convention on Civil Aviation (Chicago Convention)*. Chicago: International Civil Aviation Organization. The original copy of the agreement can be found at: www.icao.int/publications/Documents/7300_orig.pdf.
ICAO. (2013a). *Assistance to Aircraft Accident Victims and Families, 9973/486*. Montreal: International Civil Aviation Organization.
ICAO. (2013b). *Assistance to Aircraft Accident Victims and Families, Doc 9998/499*. Montreal: International Civil Aviation Organization.
ICAO. (2013c). *Policy on Assistance to Aircraft Accident Victims and Their Families: 1st Ed. Doc 9998*. Montreal: International Civil Aviation Organization.
ICAO. (2016). *Annex 9 to the Convention on International Civil Aviation Organization: 16th Ed. Facilitation*. Montreal: International Civil Aviation Organization.
ICAO. (2018). *Manual on the Regulation of International Air Transport, Doc 9626*. Montreal: International Civil Aviation Organization.
ICAO. (2021a). *Annex 13 to the Convention on International Civil Aviation Organization: 12th Ed. Aircraft Accident and Incident Investigation*. Montreal: International Civil Aviation Organization.
ICAO. (2021b). *Safety Report*. Montreal: International Civil Aviation Organization.
Montreal Agreement. The Convention for the Unification of certain Rules for International Travel. (1999). (Online). Available at: www.icao.int/Meetings/AirCargoDevelopmentForum-Togo/Documents/9740.pdf.

2 Planning for a Crisis

Chapter Objectives

By the end of this chapter, you will be able to:

- Understand what an airline plan is and why it is important
- Explain the key agencies that need to be included in airline plans
- Describe why a plan needs to be a *'living'* document and kept up to date
- Outline the importance of auditing plans
- Explain how the plans can be incorporated into airline exercises

Opening Quiz

1. Why do airlines have to have a crisis and emergency plan when there are so many variations of what could be a crisis?
2. Who needs to have access to the plan, and where should it be located? Electronically or hard copies?
3. How can a plan translate into training for those personnel in the airline who have a crisis and emergency role?
4. Would an airline be able to get a license to fly into the US from Europe if it did not have a detailed plan?

Glossary for this Chapter

ATC   Air Traffic Control
CMC   Crisis Management Centre
IATA International Air Transport Association
ICAO International Civil Aviation Organization
HAC   Humanitarian Assistance Centre
HR   Human Resources
SMS   Short message service
SOPs Standard Operating Procedures
TPPs Third Party Providers

DOI: 10.4324/9781003405337-4

Chapter Introduction

In the world of aviation crisis, it is a case of *'when'* not *'if'* an aviation crisis or emergency will happen. Of course, the challenge is understanding and recognising what a crisis is and how to handle it. Not all crises (especially in aviation) need an *'all hands on deck'* approach. Some can be dealt with quickly, such as a delay due to technical issues or weather disruption, and some need far more input from the organisation, i.e., an airborne incident or a take-off issue.

To ensure a clear understanding, it is crucial to define the key terms to be used. For the terms of this chapter, we will define a crisis as *an event that has the potential to significantly impact the airline/airport.*

Plans need to include all of the range of possible scenarios, and this includes disaster management for the worst-case scenarios. Disaster management is defined as '*a series of interrelated activities, including processes related to impact, response, recovery, development, prevention, mitigation and preparedness*' (Saputra, Satrio & Veronica, 2018). The planning stage of an aviation disaster is about being prepared for potential scenarios and planning the actions to take.

A crisis can be a slow-burn issue that, if not handled correctly and in a timely manner, can build into something much bigger. An example of this is an event on board, such as a disturbance by several passengers that is recorded via a mobile and uploaded to social media. A slow or inadequate public response from the airline follows, and the pressure builds, making it 'viral' when it really could have been handled much better initially. The key point is that to plan for a crisis takes not only plans to follow but also training, immersion in the world of crisis management and knowledge of what to do in the event of an aviation crisis.

No one is born to know what to do in a full-blown crisis. That is why there is training and plans. The other point to consider is that no two crises are the same. They may share elements of similarity such as location, aircraft and incident type, but they will always have a unique feeling to them because of those involved, passengers, families and authorities who manage them.

Understanding an Aviation Crisis and Emergency Plan

A plan is a record of the actions to be taken and by whom when a crisis occurs. This sounds easy to complete, but it is a challenge to keep it current. The previous chapter reviewed the various laws and regulations that airlines and airports need to follow. An example is the Family Assistance Act (1996/2000), where to obtain a license to fly into, out of or over the signatory's airspace, airlines need to submit a fully detailed plan (amongst other documentation). Airline and airport plans need to include all the collaborative agencies and authorities and work towards specific scenarios. There are so many agencies and parties involved that need to be written into plans that it is an ever-changing and living document.

An airline plan can also cover other related areas such as a health emergency (infection such as Ebola or Covid, etc.) and other emergencies. For the purpose of this chapter, the main focus is on full-scale aviation disasters, but for more information on health emergencies, the International Air Transport Association (IATA) website is an excellent source (IATA, 2018).

The Family Assistance Act (1996/2000) requires all airlines to have a plan that is submitted to the Department of Transport (or local equivalent) BEFORE a license can be granted. The challenge is ensuring the plan remains accurate, with vital information kept up to date and with the ever-changing roles of personnel that aviation encounters. That is why aviation plans should only have roles included and not names. This makes it less challenging to keep plans current.

An airline crisis and emergency plan needs to be broad enough to be valuable for each aviation crisis but not so complicated that no one understands it or, more likely, ignores it and does their own thing.

A plan is a legal requirement under ICAO Annex 13 (2021) requiring an airline or airport to have a plan that is audited, exercised and current. However, having an engaged organisational culture that wants one is another thing. Every airline needs a senior leadership champion. Someone who will fight for budgets, expenditures, training courses and resources. Without it, airlines run the risk of simply having a plan that collects dust on a shelf. The challenge is always trying to persuade a board and investors to invest in a plan for risk and resilience for something that everyone hopes will never need to be put into practice while they are there and they see no 'return on investment'. The plan needs to match the probable outcomes of a crisis and include costs for resources. This needs to be updated frequently to ensure it is both relevant and legal.

Building a Crisis Culture

In aviation, safety is everything. A safety culture is a prerequisite mindset for everyone who works in the organisation. A crisis mindset is not so easy to build. Perhaps it is because it means, if needed, the safety part didn't work quite as well as hoped. Perhaps it is because someone may have made a mistake or, in fact, a hundred other elements that come together for a crisis. What is needed to be a successful 'crisis mindset' organisation that responds well to a crisis, is trusted by customers and investors to respond well, and is trusted by the authorities is the same culture of crisis as safety. It is part and parcel of the everyday conversations and not seen as separate.

Some of the best airlines in the world have deeply embedded crisis cultures. Where it is okay to talk about crisis and where people engage with the crisis process. Building a crisis culture in an organisation is a core building block from which good responses are born.

One of the ways to plan is to ensure that the airline is building local relationships with groups, companies and authorities so that learning can be shared. When undertaking exercises, the best airlines also invite local hotel managers to take part so they understand what an HAC is and what help their hotel can give. This is especially important if the hotel is located near an airport as the likelihood of being used as an HAC either as a temporary measure for transferring passengers from the airport or as part of a more formal operational plan is quite high.

Inviting embassy staff, suppliers, local authorities, and the Foreign and Commonwealth Office to exercises, training sessions or meetings to understand the airline and airport plans can be beneficial; in fact, anyone who might take an interest in and be a useful partner to the airline or who might be pivotal to a response.

A plan needs to ensure there are Standard Operating Procedures or SOPS so that each role has a detailed list of tasks and actions that need to be completed, with a timeframe. Often, a role is associated with a linked role in the operation which automatically means it is vital for a crisis management team, i.e., engineering or HR. It is the role that is important and not the name of the individual. Most plans avoid putting names to roles; however, the reality is contacting people when there is a response means there needs to be a name and a contact number. This can be kept separate to avoid having to rewrite the SOP every time someone leaves or changes roles.

Keeping SOPs simple, straightforward and easy to follow in a high-pressure environment is vital for response success. All too often, airlines make the procedures for activation and response too complicated so that only a handful of people can really understand what to do. This makes training and exercising even more important. According to Masys (2004), complicated

Table 2.1 Requirements for roles within a plan

Requirements to Consider	Role	Notes
Checklist for each role	Each role should have its own checklist that is easy to find and easy to follow	Will not always cover all eventualities but can be used as a useful guide to structure the response
Equipment	What does each role need? What is generic, and what is specific?	Where will it be stored? Is the equipment up to date, e.g., laptops? Can it be easily accessed?
Scenarios	What scenarios does the plan need to include? Or no scenarios?	Ensuring the plans are a structure to cover all possible scenarios is impossible; needs to cover the main ones, though
Location	The plan needs to include the location of the CMC and contingency locations	If the CMC is airside, having one landside is a solid contingency
Changes to personnel	Who is new to the crisis team? Who needs extra training? Who needs a '*refresher*'?	Ensuring the plans are fully understood by all and the roles are clear
Changes to the airline	Does the plan still fit the airline business plan or model?	New locations, e.g., long haul, new aircraft, new business model to a low-cost one
Version control	Who controls this, and how is it communicated?	How are the version controls managed to ensure everyone has read them and understood them?

procedures and lack of training can lead to a longer-term problem of lack of real understanding of what to do in a full aviation emergency response.

When there is an accident and a team for the Crisis Management Centre (CMC) needs to activate, having a planned procedure to do this is vital. It sounds really simple, but keeping up with new mobile numbers, names and roles in a dynamic aviation environment could actually take up a full-time position. This goes back to the crisis culture in an airline so that those people who have an active role during a crisis understand how important it is to update contact details; working with HR and their systems can help alleviate the challenges of chasing people. There is no point calling the Chief Engineer on his mobile when an accident occurs to find he has changed his phone number but not told HR or the Emergency Response Manager. The authorities will not take this as an adequate excuse. This is something that can be adapted to an HR task, so the airline can benefit from updates that personnel are required to do anyway. Table 2.1 offers an overview of the kinds of requirements that may be considered a priority in an airline emergency response plan and the associated roles.

How to activate

Having a flow that clearly sets out who, when, and where is crucial for success when the time comes to activate a plan. Someone must get *'the ball rolling'*; it could be the Operations Manager, Emergency Response Manager or anyone else who is on duty and has the responsibility for activating personnel. Usually the call comes in from either Air Traffic Control (ATC) or Operations from a different location, or even media in some rare cases.

How to activate can also be challenging. The most straightforward way is a mobile phone SMS/WhatsApp® process, but that only works if everyone updates their phone numbers in the plan every time they change their phone or check their SMS. The flow of activation is explained in more detail in Chapter 3.

 Tip

Having a clear process that links HR, IT and Operations so that any updated phone numbers and emails automatically go to all three departments can be helpful. Making sure it's someone's role to regularly (monthly) check for new numbers, etc., is essential to make sure the process of activation works when it needs to.

Finally, testing the activation process during training or exercises is important so that everyone involved understands the process and can engage with it. All exercises should involve some sort of activation process so it becomes a familiar action. This process should also be tested outside working hours, i.e., Sunday afternoons or at night, to see how resilient the process actually is.

Example

The Thailand Tsunami happened on Boxing Day (26 December) in 2004. This was a national holiday in many countries. Several airlines had passengers and staff impacted by the disaster and activated their CMCs and staff. Unfortunately, many staff were absent on leave and may not have been in the location of the airline CMC.

Having a roster whereby individuals were *'on duty'* to ensure they were available and had their phones switched on helped, but then access to flights and transport generally was a challenge for the critical staff and meant CMCs (in some cases) had to run with reduced staff until other staff could attend.

Ensuring all kinds of scenarios, such as national holidays and contingency for lack of travel capacity, can minimise the negative impact these types of events can have on plans.

Planning for Absence

Everyone deserves a holiday at some point in the year. As the previous example illustrates, crises and emergencies do not always happen Monday to Friday between 0900–1700. Having a contingency plan for activation out of hours and considering absence is important. All roles and responsibilities need a deputy that can step in and take over easily so that all kinds of absences, from holidays to illness, do not negatively impact the need to activate for an emergency. This means deputies should take part in exercises and training so they understand what they are supposed to do if required to step in.

No airline can completely be 100% ready for a crisis or emergency, but all airlines should aspire to get as close as they can possibly be by understanding where they might have gaps and working hard to minimise them.

Other Challenges for Planning

 Observation

I once went to an exercise to audit an airline in Europe, and the staff IDs did not work to access the headquarters outside working hours. The exercise was at night, and no one could get in. By the time security had verified that the staff needed access and had let everyone in so the airline team had access to the CMC, it was nearly two hours after the first person had arrived. These are good challenges to iron out before any activation.

Table 2.2 Tasks and actions for key aspects of the plan

Action or Task in the Plan	Responsibility or Role
Updating all contact numbers	Everyone who is involved in being part of a crisis team, but mainly HR processes
Updating the procedures in the plan	Usually the Emergency Response Manager
Checking the laptops for the latest updates/upgrades	Usually the Emergency Response Manager, but it could be a delegated task, i.e., IT or Deputy Response Manager
Setting up room ready for activation as per the plan	Everyone who might have to work in the CMC. Make it part of an exercise for this one action alone
Training the plan/roles	Emergency Response Manager or Deputy
Exercising the plan	Emergency Response Manager or Deputy
Updating the plan post-exercise	Emergency Response Manager or Deputy

This is an example of a simple but significant challenge that no one had considered, and luckily, it happened during an exercise. Knowing who needs access to a building, specific rooms and even kit is essential to being efficient and understanding the responsibilities of the airline prior to an emergency. If the kit needed to be set up in a CMC located 20 minutes away or airside at an airport, this will not work during an activation. If laptops are not kept updated regularly and automatically start updating when started during an activation, this will delay the initial processes. There are timelines around who needs to do what and when that needs to be included and clearly understood in the plan, and it is not acceptable to tell a government official that the required paperwork will be with them as soon as all the laptops have finished updating themselves!

Table 2.2 offers an overview of the kinds of actions and tasks that might need to be managed on a regular basis and whose responsibility it might be.

 Tip

Make sure there is an alternative location identified and tested just in case the first choice of a CMC cannot be accessed for any reason. This is especially true if the CMC is located in a building located many miles from the airport or on the airport itself. Not necessarily airside, but if an emergency takes place at an airport, it is likely the local police or military may shut access, and therefore, knowing there is a local building or hotel that could be used is vital for quick and efficient setting up. The same is true for kit. If possible and finances allow, having two or splitting one kit into two in two locations can save time initially.

Audits

All plans and exercises need to be regularly audited to know if they work and offer feedback to improve. This is a regulated action by the authorities. An audit can be undertaken internally, and it is encouraged that this forms part of every exercise and even training session. Gathering feedback from participants and having an objective observer really helps with identifying gaps and potential issues to develop. Family Associations or TPPs with experience in understanding plans can help the airline to develop understanding or confidence in the plans.

Inviting an external auditor to do the same does cost money but is worth it as they can audit the plan and also understand where improvements can be made. All plans must have an audit to ensure they remain current and legal against any changing regulations or legislation by the aviation authorities.

Most airlines work directly or indirectly with a contracted TPP, and they can perform this external role. It also helps to build an understanding and relationship with the TPP so they know the plan and the roles before they have to respond to an emergency for the airline.

Testing the Plan through Exercises

Airline emergency plans need to be tested and exercised once a year. To do this does not require a huge and expensive exercise with a cast of thousands playing roles. It can be a regular but much smaller exercise, taking a key element and testing to see the resilience. It is not to catch people out but more to look for areas of development, skills gaps, strengths and areas to work on for more understanding. If an airline can join a fuller airport exercise and at the same time activate their emergency plans, it offers a *'real life'* feeling to it that helps with making those involved understand the importance of what they may have to do.

Bringing in other related parties such as TPPs, the local hotel manager, local authorities or emergency services to work together and test the plan can be hugely beneficial.

Testing the Plans with Third Party Providers

Airline and airport plans should be tested with contracted TPPs involved so that the working relationship can be built before having to activate for real. Understanding each company's culture, the people who will be involved, undertaking joint training and exercises all help to ensure that the two parties can work together in a positive way when they have to do so.

TPPs also bring lots of field experience that can help with guidance and advice for the plans. They also bring an understanding of the pressures that crisis teams are under and can often offer an air of *'calm'* during an exercise.

Having the two teams know each other before they have to activate is often the key to a successful response operation. The trust has already been tested and built, the airline culture is understood by both parties and they know how each other works.

 Observation

Having worked with lots of clients of various languages and cultures (through working for a TPP), the most successful operations have been when I understood how my role fitted into the airline client's plans and where I could add my capability to what they already had and knowing we all trusted each other. This does not happen overnight; it took years of getting to know the clients and working with them to train their staff, undertake exercises and be *'familiar'* with them. When the call came in to activate, we all knew our roles and became one team, not two.

Conclusions

It is a legal requirement for all airlines to have a well-developed plan that includes roles, responsibilities and actions required. The best airlines in the world are the ones that develop a crisis culture in the organisation so that everyone feels they have a part to play and engage with the plans. Testing the plans regularly allows for areas of development to be targeted and means when the time comes, the plans are not just a mystery written by someone who left eight years ago and where none of the contact details and roles mean anything anymore. They are *'living'* documents that everyone who has to use them understands, engages with and, more importantly, uses on a regular basis.

Key Points from this Chapter

- To obtain a license to fly into, out of or over signatories of the Family Assistance Act (1996/2000), all airlines must submit a detailed and accurate plan to the Department of Transport (or local alternative). If key details change, it is the airline's responsibility to update that plan and make sure the one submitted is both accurate and current. An example could be a change to the contracted TPP or new locations for flights
- All roles assigned to staff should have a deputy that takes part in training and exercises to ensure there are no gaps during vacation or absence through illness
- Aviation is a 24/7 operation, so accidents do not always happen between 0900–1700 Monday to Friday. Having plans that cover outside core hours must include access to buildings, security access and a roster for knowing who is on duty
- SOPs are similar to checklists used in aviation by ground staff and crew. They help the person undertaking the role to know what to do, when to do it, how to do it and where to do it. They are a structure to help teams working under pressure to follow steps and not forget anything they must cover. They need to be flexible enough to cover most scenarios but contain enough detail to help the person reading them understand what they should achieve at each step
- Exercising plans should include non-transport scenarios such as hotel explosions or natural disasters, as passengers and crew could be involved. Testing crisis roles with non-transport scenarios can build confidence and capability to work outside *'comfort zones'*
- Building relationships with TPPs and other likely agencies and authorities through joint training and exercises build resilience and adaptability for real activation
- Audits for plans should be regular, external and recorded. Any feedback on development should be actioned and discussed

---

Case Study 2 – Southwest Airlines Flight 1380

On a New York to Dallas flight, the Boeing 737 had a left-hand side engine failure followed by a decompression at a height of approximately 30,000 feet. It had left New York at 1103 and was 30 minutes into the flight. During the engine failure, parts of the engine cowl embedded into the fuselage and resulted in the loss of a cabin window and a sudden loss of pressure. There were 144 passengers on board and five crew. Tragically, one passenger died following fatal injuries, and eight more suffered minor injuries.

The flight crew made an emergency landing in Philadelphia within 30 minutes. This was deemed appropriate by the NTSB in their final report.

One of the recommendations from the NTSB report was to ensure cabin crew were trained to remain seated during an emergency landing.

Southwest used a plan dating back to 2004 in its origin. It was noted it had been updated regularly and was used to train the airline executives as well as being used as a basis for exercises.

The fact that the plan was a *'living document',* in that everyone understood it, it was trained regularly, updated as required and exercised as well as audited, meant that when it was needed, the plan worked. Everyone involved knew what they had to do and were able to follow the SOPs without confusion.

Figure 2.1 NTSB official inspecting the engine and cowl of Southwest 1380
Reproduced courtesy of the NTSB

As you can see in Figure 2.1, the damage from the engine failure for Southwest 1380 was considerable.

Case Study Questions

1. Do you consider this to be a typical scenario for airlines to train and exercise? How could Southwest have exercised this realistically?
2. What kind of feedback from the flight deck and cabin crew would have been helpful after the event for the crisis teams to consider for their plans?
3. How would the recommendation from the NTSB to have cabin crew remain seated throughout an emergency landing be communicated through training?

Quiz

Take a few minutes to complete this quiz to check your understanding of this chapter.

1. The Family Assistance Act (1996/2000) requires airlines to have an up-to-date plan for a crisis. True or false?
2. How do airlines need to check their emergency plans once written to make sure they are still valid?

3. If the CMC is in a restricted location, i.e., an airport office, where else should airlines consider a backup location in their plans?
4. Why does each key role in the CMC need a deputy who is trained as well?
5. What would the difference be between an internal audit and an external audit?
6. Which ICAO Annex is linked to the requirements of having a '*current*' plan?
7. How does having a good relationship with a TPP help airlines during an activation?

References and Additional Reading

IATA. (2018). *Emergency Response Plan*. Public Health Emergency. Can be found at: www.iata.org/contentassets/f1163430bba94512a583eb6d6b24aa56/airlines-erp-checklist.pdf.

ICAO. (2021). *Annex 13 to the Convention on International Civil Aviation Organization: 12th Ed. Aircraft Accident and Incident Investigation*. Montreal: International Civil Aviation Organization.

Masys, A. (2004). Aviation Accident Aetiology: Catastrophe Theory Perspective. *Disaster Prevention and Management*, 13 (1) pp. 33–38. https://doi.org/10.1108/09653560410521670.

Saputra, M. A., Satrio, R., & Veronica, A. (2018). Airport Disaster Management Plan Towards Natural Disasters. *Advances in Engineering Research (AER)*, 147. https://doi.org/10.2991/grost-17.2018.36.

Part II

Activation, Deployment and Specific Roles

3 Crisis Management Centre (CMC)

Chapter Objectives

By the end of this chapter, you will be able to:

* Explain what a Crisis Management Centre is
* Outline the initial activation process for working in a Crisis Management Centre
* Describe the initial tasks and actions for staff working in the Crisis Management Centre
* Understand the initial timescales for actions to be completed as per legislation
* Explain what a Telephone Enquiry Centre is and what it does
* Describe the timelines for when the Telephone Enquiry Centre should be ready to take calls

Opening Quiz

1. What is a CMC?
2. How are airlines notified of an accident?
3. What is a TEC?
4. What are the two team roles working within a TEC, and how do they differ?
5. Give three examples of who needs access to a confirmed passenger manifest.

Glossary for this Chapter

AAIB   Air Accident Investigation Branch
ATC   Air Traffic Control
CAA   Civil Aviation Authority
CMC   Crisis Management Centre
FAA   Federal Aviation Authority
HAC   Humanitarian Assistance Centre
H&S   Health and Safety
IMC   Incident Management Centre
NTSB   National Transportation Safety Bureau
SFO   San Francisco three letter aviation code
TEC   Telephone Enquiry Centre
TPP   Third Party Provider

DOI: 10.4324/9781003405337-6

Chapter Introduction

Airlines are legislated to ensure they are able to respond successfully to an accident. Both ICAO Annex 13 (2021) and the Family Assistance Act (1996/2000) regulate the basic structure and requirements of a location set aside for managing the response by the airline.

A Crisis Management Centre (CMC) is a dedicated room or one that can be quickly converted to manage the initial operations of an accident. It is resourced by trained staff of the airline who have specific roles that are clearly defined but work together. Cilliers (1998) suggests that crisis management sits outside routine management and outside aviation operations.

Of course, CMCs do not always need to be a set-aside office; they can be an office that can convert to the CMC at a time of need, such as a board room, but this brings its own challenges. Any room used for multiple purposes needs to be cleared quickly and needs to have equipment stored securely with quick access, not a key that only one person who lives far away has (for example).

The airline emergency plan should be readily available both in digital and hard copy. Staff assigned roles should have been trained, and an exercise (once per year) achieved, to capture learning and development (see Chapter 2 for more details). The reputation of the airline can be negatively impacted if the response to the accident is poor, slow or disorganised. Alternatively, if the airline responds well to an accident and can demonstrate a solid understanding of what is required when an accident occurs, this can actually positively impact the reputation of the airline (Coombs & Holliday, 2004).

All equipment in the CMC needs to be checked regularly, and this is often the role of the airline Emergency Response Manager. Laptops should be kept updated in terms of upgrades and serviceability, etc. Opening up the CMC is a core exercise that should be familiar to all those who might be asked to work there. It needs to be opened by anyone on the team, as the first person to arrive at the CMC assumes control until others arrive.

Notification Flow

When an accident occurs, it is the responsibility of the State of Occurrence to notify all of the relevant parties. The relevant parties would include:

- State of Design
- State of Manufacture
- State of Registry
- State of Operator
- ICAO if the mass is above 2250KG (in essence, a commercial aircraft)

This should be undertaken by telephone and in one of the agreed working languages of ICAO, but not necessarily in English. All parties should be informed of the numbers on board and whether there are any '*dangerous goods*' being carried as cargo.

Of course, the State of Occurrence may not be aware of an accident or may not have the infrastructure or capability to notify all of these States, in which case allowances are made for the State of Registry or the State of Operator to be able to forward on all of the notifications including vital information needed to understand the situation.

As Figure 3.1 outlines, parties require a certain amount of '*confirmed*' information at the time of notification. Not all elements may be available initially, but can be passed on when the information is known.

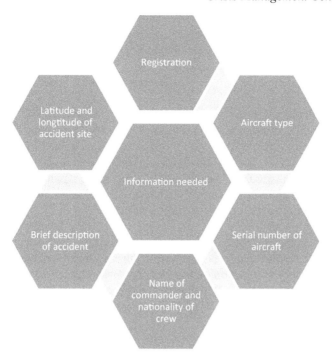

Figure 3.1 Required initial information from 'State of Occurrence'

Model adapted from ICAO Annex 13 (2013a)

How a Response Begins

The State of Operator will usually be informed via the on-duty Operations Manager at the airline. The on-duty Manager will call the Emergency Response Manager, and the process of activating the crisis begins. If the accident occurs within the airspace of a local airport, then the accident could be activated via ATC, who would also contact the on-duty Operations Manager. Airlines should continue to run a scheduled operation alongside an accident unless told not to do so by the authorities, i.e., NTSB,[1] Federal Aviation Administration (FAA)[2] or Civil Aviation Authority (CAA)[3] in the event of a potential aircraft fault, e.g., grounded aircraft such as after the two B737MAX crashes for Lion Air JT610 (October 2018) and Ethiopian Airlines ET302 (March 2019) which led to the temporary grounding of the B373MAX fleet worldwide.

This means the CMC should be self-sufficient in terms of personnel and equipment, and personnel working there should be able to do so and not also be required to be part of the normal operations as well. This can be challenging, especially in lean airlines such as low-cost or ultra-low-cost ones. Having a good relationship with the contracted TPP is crucial to be able to carry on with a form of operational schedule AND manage an accident that may well need extra skilled personnel to support the CMC.

The CMC should only ever be populated by the relevant personnel who are trained and understand their role. Usually, with slightly more information available than other parties at this point, the first and key job of the CMC is to start the process of informing the relevant parties, as per the Family Assistance Act (1996/2000) and ICAO Annex 13 (2021), and set in motion those teams who may be needed to deploy, i.e., Go Teams and Special Assistance Teams.

The initial task that the first person to arrive must undertake is to activate any TPP support they may need. This is usually an outsourced contract with a disaster management organisation to supply services such as forensic identification, search and recovery of the crash site and managing the Humanitarian Assistance Centre (HAC). Not all airlines have this outsourced contract with a TPP, but most do. Few airlines can run a scheduled operation AND an accident at the same time.

The Telephone Enquiry Centre (TEC) must be activated in the initial phase as well. Be that an external call centre contracted to support the airline during a crisis via the TPP or an internally trained team. Once activated from the list of on-duty contacts, the TEC is required to be up and running in one hour from the call. Obviously, this will be a minimal team initially, but they must be ready to take calls in that time. Many TECs now have a remote working system that allows for call takers to be up and running from home within minutes. A fully seated call centre is not necessarily required except for large-scale disasters.

The relevant aviation authorities must also be informed. These include the CAA, FAA and NTSB/AAIB. This emphasises the preference, where possible, for a pre-set up standalone office space to have all the relevant phone numbers and contacts already populated on whiteboards and on laptops set up for the sole purpose of running a crisis. This is why pre-populated or formulated whiteboards can work so well in the initial phase of an airline crisis. Note in Figure 3.2 that the NTSB also includes whiteboards as crucial equipment for the CMC.

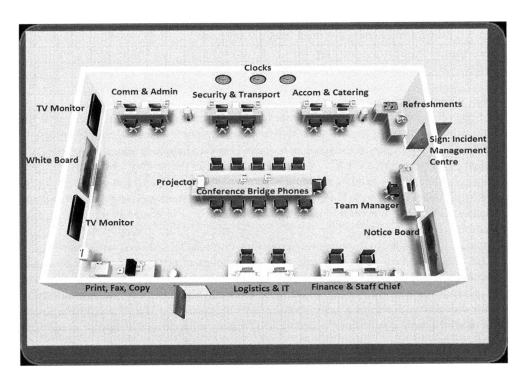

Figure 3.2 NTSB suggested setup for a CMC

Reproduced courtesy of NTSB

The first person to arrive at the CMC should be able to populate the following information straightaway, which they should have easily to hand:

- Flight no. and destination/arrival airport
- Numbers of passengers on board
- Aircraft type and registration
- Crew details – probably numbers only at this early point
- TEC toll-free number
- Potentially dangerous goods in the hold

Equipment needed in the CMC

The CMC does not require a huge amount of equipment. The list of equipment essential in the CMC is not exhaustive but should include the following items:

1. Laptops set up for easy access and with templates already available, i.e., prepopulated Excel or specific programmes used for data collation and sharing. There needs to be enough for all key roles and staff working in the CMC, and staff should NOT use their own laptops for an activation to ensure the information and data gathered on the laptops remain there as part of any investigation, security, inquiry or review into working procedures.
2. Whiteboards and pens, etc. Although aviation is, by default, a highly technical industry, having whiteboards is deemed an essential piece of equipment. This is for several reasons. Being self-sufficient, the CMC needs to run even in the event of electrical or WIFI outages. Whiteboards also act as a point of focus for everyone in the room for vital information that is updated regularly by a log keeper.

   - Time of activation and time of incident local time and at CMC and date
   - Flight no.
   - Registration of aircraft
   - Type of aircraft
   - Type of disaster (if known), i.e., natural, terrorist, accident, etc.
   - Departure airport and destination – location of accident if in between airports
   - Codeshare or Alliance contact details
   - Numbers of passengers and crew – broken down by adults, children, infants, etc.
   - Nationalities of those involved
   - Confirmed survivors and types of injuries, etc. Can include uninjured and those not accounted for
   - Hospitals involved and contact details
   - Location of mortuary and contact details
   - Contact details for National Transportation Safety Board (NTSB) Air Accident Investigation Branch (AAIB)[4] and other relevant agencies, i.e., contracted TPPs
   - Timings for press statements and *'tweets'*, etc.
   - Security issues, i.e., dangerous goods in the hold, explosives, etc.
             (Adapted from International Criminal Police Organisation (INTERPOL, 2019)

As the accident progresses, the information will change to include confirmed deceased and numbers of Go Team and Special Assistance Team (SAT) members deployed. As the CMC is often a high-pressure environment with noise and telephones ringing, having clearly available information on whiteboards can help with accuracy and means those working in the CMC do not have to rely on their ability to remember key information. As it changes, it also helps with consistency of information.

Other whiteboards can include names of management of the CMC, contact details and location of HAC, TEC contact number, etc.

Set up for CMC

The NTSB has an illustrative setup for a CMC. Note the inclusion of whiteboards, refreshments and TV monitors to review news channels. All relevant documentation plans and manuals should also be easily available.

Figure 3.2 offers a couple of key points. Initially, note there is one door in and out. This is a key consideration for the location of the CMC. It is no good having multiple access and egress as security is paramount in terms of information and decision-making. If the chosen room has multiple doors, consider using only one and locking the others off (within H&S procedures locally), as the CMC may well need security on the door depending on where the room is and the severity and profile of the crisis being managed.

Access to view TV screens can be useful for a variety of reasons, including keeping up with what is being said and presented by media and it can give an overview of the site itself and how survivors are being treated and triaged. That said, it can be distracting, so having images without sound is recommended. Clocks are vital for local time and location of accident time accuracy.

Flow of Information

There is a set flow to the procedures of informing the authorities and tasks to undertake. The first person into the CMC should make a note of the time on a whiteboard to start the log keeping.

Securing an Accurate Passenger Manifest

The passenger manifest is needed to confirm those who are on board the aircraft and impacted by the accident as per ICAO Doc 9973. The role of the TEC operators is NOT to issue death notices to callers, but they use the manifest for incoming calls from relatives and potentially confirm if their loved one is, in fact, on the passenger manifest. A copy should be sent to the TEC as a priority to enable them to be ready to take calls within the required one hour.

It should be noted that in recent years, the passenger manifest is often leaked to the media and can be seen on TV and social media from early on in an accident. This is regrettable and to be avoided, but if the airline representatives at the CMC have undertaken the task of *'locking down'* the manifest to make it secure, this may be something that is outside the control of the airline.

An example is Ethiopian Airlines Flight ET302 from Addis Ababa to Nairobi in 2019, which crashed, killing all on board. The passenger manifest was released to the public within minutes of the news breaking by an unknown source and caused the website to fail due to the number of people trying to get onto the site. This detracts from the TEC trying to gather initial and vital information about the loved ones on board.

The relevant authorities will also ask for a copy of the passenger manifest. As per the Family Assistance Act (1996/2000), this must be sent to them as soon as it has been confirmed to be accurate and secure and within a *'specified period of time'* (ICAO Doc 9973, 2013b, 3.2:21).[5] Best practice for this is three hours, but as soon as it can be confirmed as accurate. Accuracy is always preferred over speed in these situations.

Other interested parties that might request a passenger manifest are the police, military involved in rescue operations, hospitals receiving the injured and the TPP if travelling to the location to support. The NTSB and/or AAIB will also require a copy on request.

Activate Key Personnel

Planning to activate the Go Team and any contracted TPP should be initiated early on. They do not necessarily need to be activated immediately but rather at this stage, put on standby. This way, all those involved can have time to pack and clear any tasks or priorities that might need their attention. By placing teams on standby, it is always possible to stand them down later on if not required, but knowing the teams are ready to go when needed saves time.

In terms of process, activating the Go Team first is a priority. They may need travel arrangements made unless there is an aircraft from the airline leaving. Consider if vaccinations (see Chapter 4) and visas are required. However, before any Go Team is activated, the local situation should be assessed via the Foreign and Commonwealth Office (or State equivalent) and local sources such as embassies or consulates.

An example of when not sending a Go Team might be appropriate would be in a conflict war zone or an ongoing terrorist attack, i.e., the beach attacks in Suisse that impacted TUI in 2015. It might be too dangerous to send personnel there and also might add to the ongoing challenges for the local authorities. The next priority is to send out the first statement.

The Family Assistance Act (1996/2000) requires the airline at CMC to release an initial *'tweet'* within 15 minutes of notification. This is a holding statement that acknowledges there is an accident unfolding, that the airline is aware of it and that more information will be offered (state when). If a toll-free number is released, that should also be included in the statement along with any information available on the website.

The initial *'tweet'* template can be found in Chapter 8 on Crisis Communications.

The initial *'tweet'* and subsequent statements for the press and social media should be released to media outlets and put on social media sites for the airline. This means that IT or Crisis Communications personnel should be involved in the CMC initially to ensure these can be done within the timeframes.

 Observation

Check who has access to change and/or upload social media notifications. Are they part of the CMC team? Make sure they understand this element of their role and, if the time comes, can execute the process quickly and efficiently. This applies to IT and the website being changed to a dark site[6] with elements removed or updated, i.e., a ticker tape with the toll-free number. Having a six-hour delay while the right person is found to undertake this is not acceptable and will result in criticism from outside observers, families and survivors. Take time to know who the best contact is to work with and train them, include them in exercises and make them part of the CMC team.

Finally, does an outside hours phone message need to be changed, directing people to the toll-free number and website for information?

Communications may also include an internal email to staff keeping them up to date on the situation (much the same wording as the initial statement) but also to direct worried staff to their managers or an agreed contact for support. Engaging staff early is essential for their wellbeing (see Chapter 8 for examples).

Once the CMC is opened and staff have arrived, the positions can be organised. Making sure all roles are covered is essential, and this is something that pre-accident exercises and training can help with. Roles in the CMC may not be the same as the roles that individuals have in their everyday lives. The transition needs to be learned and practiced before having to do it for real. Having flexibility is important for the smooth running of the CMC, so training several people for the same role is essential in case individuals are on leave, unwell or have left the airline. Having a *'single point of failure'* in the CMC due to missing personnel will quickly diminish the effectiveness of managing an accident.

Overview of Key Roles in the CMC

Log keeping

It is important that all notes taken around meetings and decisions are both accurate and kept for the investigating authorities and any possible court proceedings as part of an inquiry, as they may be asked for as evidence. This is a key role in the CMC, but of course, the first person who arrives might not be the Log Keeper. They should, however, start the process by making notes about key areas such as arrival time, when the passenger manifest was requested to be *'locked down'*, when the TPP was put on standby or activated, when the Go Team was put on standby or activated, etc. This can be done via a notebook or the whiteboard initially and then transferred when the Log Keeper arrives.

All laptop stations should include a pad and pen for jotting down key timings and names, etc. Again, note you can have technological systems to cover this embedded in the airline emergency systems used, but for memory jogging and as people are often juggling multiple requests, an old-fashioned notebook and pen is really an essential element of accurate note-taking in the CMC.

The Log Keeper is a vital part of the team and needs to be trained to understand the importance of having accurate, updated and current information laid out in a way that is clear and straightforward to read. ONLY the log keeper should alter the whiteboards; information that needs to go on the boards should always pass through the Log Keeper. To ensure consistency and coverage, the Log Keeper role should be a team that can take over quickly and efficiently as shifts finish. Often, this role falls to admin teams that are expert in this type of data and information gathering and accurate reporting.

Crisis Director

The Crisis Director is the most senior person who is trained to make decisions whilst the CMC is operational. Note this is not necessarily the MOST senior person in the organisation, and anyone working in the CMC should understand (through training) that the role of Crisis Director in the CMC outranks the roles in normal operations.

This role should be an experienced member of staff, usually with specific skills and training in this area or experience running a CMC. They are required to make decisions about Who?

What? When? Where? etc., based often on not enough information (as they would wish to have) to make fast decisions that might need to be changed once extra information comes in.

They must be calm, able to communicate well and have enough gravitas to work with senior management, national or international authorities and potentially the media.

Crisis Deputy Director

This role is more of an operational management role that ensures the CMC runs smoothly on a day-to-day basis. They can deputise for the Crisis Director but have more management rather than a leadership role. They can work more closely with the various teams within the CMC, such as IT, HR, logistics, engineering, etc., so that the Crisis Director can be freed up to be more strategic and work with senior leadership and authorities.

Again, they need to be experienced and confident at running a high-pressure team and making operational decisions without needing to ask the Crisis Director. These two roles work closely together and should train and exercise together when possible as part of the airline plans.

Logistics

This role (or more usually a team) works with the Go Team (and others) to ensure they get to the destination by whatever transport or route is the quickest. Also, any equipment that needs to be deployed with them. The equipment may already be in set kits, and knowing what is in each kit is vital for this team. They also need to understand weights, the export process and what paperwork is required for cargo. Often taken from an *'operational'* or *'ground dispatch'* type role given the need to understand cargo and aircraft documentation for export regulations and weight distribution on aircraft, etc.

Crisis Centre Manager

This is the role that decides who will activate, to where and when. They need to understand the teams and their skills, capabilities and experience, so having a working knowledge of the volunteers at the airline and being involved in their training and exercises will help determine who is the most appropriate to activate for a particular situation.

This role will also have a good working relationship with the TPP and will be liaising with them about how many of their team might need to deploy and where to. They undertake the coordination of the various teams and ensure the wellbeing of the teams within the CMC. This could be part of the *'emergency management team'*, *'SAT Team Manager'* or a similar role.

IT/HR

These roles can be overlooked in setting up and training a CMC team. They are essential parts of the team as they have to ensure the whole crisis operation remains on track and efficient.

IT needs to ensure any issues with technology and equipment can be quickly and easily fixed, and HR needs to work on creating rosters for an ongoing operation, find contact details for the crew, etc., where they may be the only people who have access to the systems or information required. Including them in all training and exercises is essential. HR also needs to have access to all HR processes and not have to ask for permission due to *'limited access'*. IT needs to have knowledge of how to activate the *'dark site'* and work with Sales and Marketing teams to switch off promotional messages.

Crisis Communication Manager and Team

Often, crisis communications can be an internal team to the airline or, more usually, an externally retained team, either as part of the TPP or as a '*standalone*' organisation with the required expertise in crisis communications.

This team will ensure the initial '*tweet*' and press statement has been released to the appropriate channels and in the most appropriate medium. They will also work on all subsequent statements, press conferences and social media messages either by posting or having an overview of what is being posted (see Chapter 8).

Administration

Often overlooked, this team is vital for the success of the CMC. This team organises all of the information that needs to be gathered, stored and filed accurately for use later on by investigating authorities or inquests.

Each person on the manifest will be given their own file ref. number, and any information gathered on paper will be stored according to the person to whom it relates. This is called '*a victim file*' or similar. Every single name on the manifest will be given its own file. Any electronic information will be overviewed by the admin team to ensure accuracy, i.e., spelling and location.

Table 3.1 offers an overview of the various general roles, responsibilities, and interactions for an aviation accident Crisis Management Centre. These can vary depending on the situation and type of aircraft or location, etc.

Activation and Deployment Process from the CMC

The use of SMS is standard for activation of key personnel for the CMC. This includes the Go Team and SAT members who may have to deploy to the location to support those impacted.

The flow of the SMS is key to a speedy initial phase of an operation and is illustrated in what follows and demonstrates why having up-to-date contact details for all relevant personnel is essential. If the details are wrong, the individual will not receive an SMS alert.

1. An SMS message is sent to all required personnel, i.e., Go Team and SATs, to ask if they are available to deploy to the location.
2. The required answer is a simple YES/NO/MAYBE.
3. The 'YES' answers will be dealt with quickly by a follow-up phone call by the CMC team (probably administration through the Crisis Centre Manager) to ascertain more details.
4. The 'NO' answers will be ignored for now. If more personnel are required later, they will be contacted again.
5. The 'MAYBE' answers are kept for later. This might mean they have caring responsibilities that need organising but could go on the following week or work challenges that need to be delegated before they can deploy. Again, these will be contacted once the initial 'YES' teams have been organised in the first phase of an operation.

The 'YES' responses will be reviewed against what HR has as their role in a crisis. This will include when they were trained, any specific qualifications, i.e., languages or ex-military, etc., or part of the trained Go Team.

Table 3.1 Roles and responsibilities of CMC staff

Role	Key Responsibilities	Interactions
Crisis Director	Overall responsibility for the CMC, decision maker for key actions, strategic leadership of operation	Authorities, Government depts., other agencies, potentially media
Crisis Deputy Director	Manages day-to-day operations in the CMC, takes strategic decisions and translates them into actions, manages team	Crisis Director, can deputise for other strategic meetings as required
Logistics	Help support the deployment of the Go Team and equipment to location	Crisis Centre Manager, potentially other airlines and cargo organisations and the TPP
Crisis Centre Manager	Activates Go team, SATs and other key personnel, makes decisions on who will deploy and when, looks after the welfare of the team and facilities in CMC	Crisis Deputy Director and HR
HR	Looks after crew families initially, ensures rosters are created for the CMC team, accesses systems and records for crew and other relevant staff, i.e., Go Team	Crisis Centre Manager, all other teams in CMC as required, rest of airline as required
IT	Ensures all technology and equipment are working to optimum capacity, supports issues and breakages, activates the *'dark site'*	Crisis Centre Manager. Sales and Marketing if promotional messages need to be halted
Crisis Communications	Retrieves and publishes all early statements and ensures answering phone messages are changed, overview of social media and other media	Crisis Centre Director and other crisis teams as required
Log Keeper	Updates all information on whiteboards, takes notes at key meetings	Crisis Centre Manager OR Crisis Director as appropriate
Administration	Ensures all information relayed is captured and stored correctly and safely in systems or platforms (as appropriate), interacts with the activation process, Go Team and SATs (for example)	HR, IT, Logistics and Crisis Centre Manager

The 'YES Team' will then be the priority for the CMC to either deploy to the location as part of the Go Team, SATs, come to the CMC to work there as part of a rostered shift or go to the airport (if relevant) to support staff there.

Different airlines have slightly different ways of activation, but they will be similar to the previously mentioned process.

The Go Team will probably be on a separate list, and they understand that as part of this team, they agree to deploy at short notice (unless on leave, etc.) and will be deployed along with any other relevant personnel at the earliest possible point, not necessarily as one team but to meet at the destination to become one team (see Chapter 4 for more details). The initial flow for activation of the CMC and those personnel involved is illustrated in Figure 3.3.

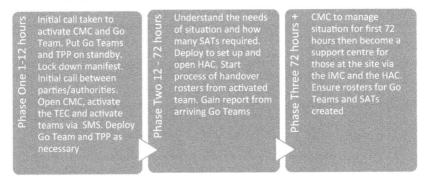

Figure 3.3 Process for initial activation and actions

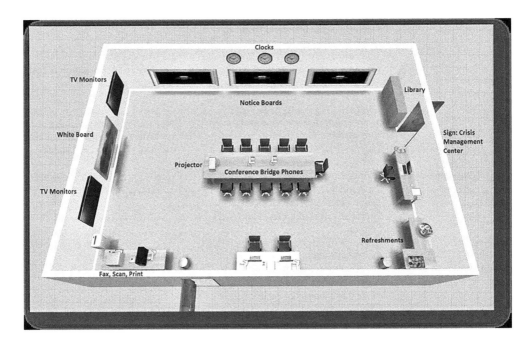

Figure 3.4 Incident Management Centre

Reproduced courtesy of the NTSB

Incident Management Centre (IMC)

The CMC takes control of managing the situation from the perspective of the airline for the time it takes for the Go Team to get to the location, the HAC to be set up and opened and SATs in position. This is usually within the first 24 hours (Phase 2 in Figure 3.3). Long enough to give teams a chance to set up and open a centre at or near the location to manage the operation there. The new airline management centre will usually be set up in the HAC to manage the day-to-day operations and is called the Incident Management Centre (IMC).

Once the IMC is set up and open, the CMC takes a more supportive role in the background, transferring decision-making and operational overview to the IMC. This is usually around 72 hours after notification but could be earlier depending on the location and size of the response

(Phase 3 of Figure 3.3). Some of the personnel from the CMC might transfer over to the IMC, but certainly, the CMC will usually, at this point, reduce resources. It should also revert to the time zone of the IMC to ensure most resources are available at times the IMC is busy. That might mean the CMC will open from 1800–1000 instead of during the day locally to support the time zone of the IMC and the operation at the location. Towards the end of an activation, when the HAC is closing down, the IMC will transfer management back to the CMC (see Chapter 11). Fig 3.5 shows that often Alliances partners can be the first to start the CMC process due to time zones and location of the accident.

The IMC should be set up to mirror the CMC. Clearly, this may not be possible if the HAC is in a hotel. Experience suggests there may need to be a compromise on setup for security. In addition to the whiteboards or flipcharts, if that's what the hotel can provide, the IMC needs to manage the Go Team and SAT movements, contact details and key meetings as part of their duty of care. Also, travel plans and incoming family members need to be met. As this information is sensitive and may be confidential, there will be a need for security to limit access to the IMC. Regard it as an extension of the airline CMC and minimise access.

Case Study 3 – Asiana 214 July 2013

Asiana 214 from South Korea clipped the San Francisco (SFO) runway wall on landing on 6 July 2013, killing three passengers.

The initial activation came from Asiana's alliance partners based at SFO. This was because of the time change in South Korea, and often alliance partners do support each other until a delegation arrives, such as the Go Team.

Figure 3.5 Asiana 214 wreckage at San Francisco airport

Attribution: Basil D Soufi, CC BY-SA 3.0 <https://creativecommons.org/licenses/by-sa/3.0>, via Wikimedia Commons

The problem was the team from South Korea did not arrive in SFO for several days. This caused issues in communication and support. Criticism of Asiana included:

1. Asiana failed to keep the families of those involved updated. They relied on the goodwill of alliance partners in SFO to do this for them.
2. It took too long to release a toll-free number for those concerned to call.
3. The senior leadership team did not arrive for nearly a week afterwards.
4. Their plans were deemed to be *'not current'*, and some contact details for key partners were out of date.

In the end, they were fined $500K for failing to undertake a required process for an accident.[7]

Telephone Enquiry Centre (TEC)

One of the crucial parts of the initial phase of response for airlines, as it is required in both ICAO Doc 9973 and the Family Assistance Act (1996/2000), is linked to the toll-free number that the airline has to release within a *'specified period of time'* according to ICAO Doc 9973 (2013b, 3.4b:21) e.g., the United Arab Emirates (UAE) specifies within *'one hour'* and this is seen to be best practice.

This means the Telephone Enquiry Centre (TEC) or more recently commonly referred to as the *'Contact Centre'* due to the variety of communication mediums available for enquiries, needs to be up and running within the agreed upon and trained timeframe. Most airlines can activate a small team that can focus on initial calls or utilise either an internal sales team call centre or a passenger call centre that they pay for in another country. Using internal staff is always a risk because of the nature of the calls that might come in and also the sheer size of the potential incoming calls. If internal staff are to be utilised initially, they need to be trained and supported for the task. According to ICAO Doc 9973, call operators should be trained and experienced in dealing with callers after an accident. This is usually why airlines tend to use specific call centres and share them so the agents can benefit from training. Having to deal with highly distressed callers and gaining the necessary information from them takes great skill and should not be undertaken by untrained personnel (Teleworldwire.com, 2022).

Toll-free number

The toll-free number must ensure that no one calling in has to endure expenses. It can, however, be challenging for countries to produce these fast enough for an event. That is why most airlines have a toll-free number retained on a monthly basis so it can be utilised whenever needed, e.g., for weather delays, hotel incidents, aircraft accidents, etc. This is especially true as the response requirements of releasing a number make it almost impossible to activate unless it is already retained by the airlines. One advantage of already having the toll-free number *'in the back pocket'* means it can be submitted with plans, used for training and exercises, gives airlines the ability to test it with alliance partners, TPP's and other agencies during these exercises and finally the number can be chosen to be easy to learn or retain.

A disadvantage is this will cost a monthly retainer. Not a huge amount, but for airlines that work within an ultra-lean business model, it just adds to the overall outgoing monthly costs.

Of course, toll-free numbers might not be possible in some regions of the world, and utilising these easy and free phone numbers may not suit all callers. That is why a range of contact avenues must be released alongside. These may include an email address, text capability, social media or website communication. These also take some of the pressure away from the TEC but, again, require additional resources to monitor and be able to be consistent with the message and data collection. One further challenge when considering a multiple range of communication channels is how the various systems *'talk'* to each other and collect information about those trying to offer and receive information about passengers. It is not always the best option to have multiple channels for communication if these independent systems collect vital information but then do not share it, so key data is missed, or relatives have to repeat information several times.

Inbound calls and outbound calls using TEC

If considering a TEC internally or trying to understand the process of a TEC externally, it is important to know there are two main teams. Those who concentrate on the public calling in to enquire about a relative or friend who may be on board using the published toll-free number and those who concentrate on calling out when notification is given that an individual is *'confirmed as involved'* on the passenger list. Remember, this does not mean a *'death notification'* but confirms the passenger's name is on the manifest.

Inbound call team

This team is the first to activate and should *'scale up'* to ensure there is enough resource to answer the calls quickly. The ability to *'scale up'* in a crisis is easier when using cloud-based systems or the use of additional emails and messages through a variety of channels (Venugopal, Li & Ray 2011). These call takers are uniquely placed to capture information about the callers that might prove to be vital for understanding who is the *'next of kin'* or the *'nearest relative to the name on the manifest'*, who may need *'extra support'*, *'who might want to come to the Humanitarian Assistance Centre (HAC)'*, etc. They can also determine languages, culture, religion, demographics and disability, all of which can support the teams who may be asked to support the families further down the road.

These teams can also *'filter'* callers who may have other priorities but want information from the TEC. Callers who might want to enquire about a future flight, those who want information but have no loved one on board, media callers and potentially more sinister callers who may have less than positive intentions, called *'crank callers'* (Harris, 2004).

An inbound media call line or email has to be available to offer the media access to the latest confirmed information through released statements or collating questions and themes useful for future conferences. The call takers will be able to transfer the media callers to the appropriate lines or avenues for information to free up vital lines for other callers.

Call takers may use a script as a framework to ensure they capture all of the most vital information. Well-trained and experienced call takers know how to converse naturally via the script without the callers feeling they are being *'processed'*. The type of information that airlines, authorities and investigators need from these inbound calls are:

1. Who is the *'next of kin or nearest relative'* OR *'decision maker'* for the family? This may not be the same person, and an example might be the next of kin could be a frail or elderly relative unable to make cognitive decisions, so the eldest child may make the decisions on behalf of the family, with their consent.
2. Who, listed on the manifest, is getting lots of calls, and who is getting fewer or none? This helps offer a picture of how many passengers can be *'confirmed on the manifest'* or *'notified they have been involved'* when planning for support either at the HAC, hospital or in the families' own homes.

Information and key data must be collected to ensure accurate links between those calling in and the passengers on the manifest. Names on the manifest are often different to passport names or names the families know them by. There may be multiple duplications of names, and time should be spent to absolutely know the link has been made. Once the *'next of kin or nearest relative'* or *'decision maker'* is identified and a solid link confirmed to the passenger name on the manifest, this can be passed over to the outbound team.

Outbound Call Team

Notification calls to the family are always managed by the outbound team. This needs very careful handling and experienced, confident call takers. It involves having all the correct information before calling the nominated family link and confirming their loved one is on the passenger manifest and '*confirmed as involved'*. This takes delicacy, diplomacy, resilience and sensitivity, as it often means the start of a traumatic journey for the families and friends. If the passenger has been injured, the family needs to know where they are and make arrangements to talk to them (if possible) or travel to the HAC or hospital.

Clearly, if the passenger *'may'* be deceased and this is never confirmed over the phone, then arrangements need to be made to plan for who will be travelling to the HAC, what arrangements need to be made, how many will be travelling and when they will be travelling. A specific travel team working closely with the airline and the CMC will usually take over here to book travel arrangements (ICAO Doc 9973, 2013b).

At this point, asking the family to bring an example for potential DNA analysis, what this might be and any other documentation that could be needed is explained to the families, i.e., a toothbrush or items of clothing (see Chapter 7 for more details).

All families or friends travelling to the HAC will need to bring identification to prove who they are and bring anything else that might be of help, i.e., dentist or doctor contact information, etc., for their loved one.

Conclusions

The CMC and TEC are core elements of the initial response by an airline to an accident. Being able to work closely together to release the toll-free number, open up the CMC and start the notification process to the authorities, as well as activate the TEC, means the response operation can stay within the requirements for initial actions. This includes any crisis communications such as the initial 'tweet' press statements, setting up the remote TEC or internal teams and working to exchange confirmed information quickly. Sending the passenger manifest to the TEC in plenty of time to open up means the first of the required regulations can be adhered to.

Both teams at the TEC need to be trained, exercised and know their role and what initial actions need to be taken.

The CMC will take the lead in managing the initial phase of a response until the IMC is set up and able to take over. The TEC will communicate closely with the CMC and then the IMC to ensure information about who is travelling to the HAC, when they are travelling and who they are linked to, giving the IMC, the HAC management and the Go Teams and SATs vital information to plan and support everyone as they need it.

Key Points from this Chapter

- Airlines need to have a toll-free number ready to go BEFORE an accident occurs due to the speed of releasing this number for concerned friends and relatives

- Most airlines 'outsource' this service to call centres due to the number of calls anticipated and the skills required to receive these types of calls
- There should be a media number available to transfer media calls and free up lines for callers
- There are two key teams in a TEC for an aviation accident. The *'inbound team'* for gathering information and the *'outbound team'* to notify families of their loved one being *'involved'*
- Establishing who is the nearest relative to the passenger name on the manifest can take time and needs accuracy over speed
- The decision maker in the family may not always be the nearest relative

Quiz

Take a few minutes to complete this quiz to check your understanding of this chapter.

1. What do CMC and IMC stand for
2. Why is it so important that contact details are kept up to date with airline HR departments or systems?
3. What does a Crisis Centre Director do? And who do they interact with?
4. If personnel respond with a 'Maybe' when messaged to activate, what might be the reasons?
5. Why does a CMC have whiteboards when there is so much technology to use?
6. What are the key role responsibilities for a Log Keeper?
7. How long does the CMC 'usually' remain on active management before the IMC takes over at the location?
8. What is the best practice timescale for a toll-free number to be available and published?
9. What are the two distinct teams of the TEC?
10. Can a 'death notification' be given from the TEC?
11. Why is it important to know who is the decision maker for a family if the next of kin is vulnerable or frail?

Exercise

ABC airlines have declared that their aircraft is missing. ATC called the on-duty Operations Manager to say that the registered aircraft Z-PLKC1 had disappeared from their radar at 2345 local time.

The Operations Manager has called the TPP to put them on standby and called the senior on-duty Emergency Response Manager to update them on the details. These contact numbers were on the board in the Operations Room, so they were easy to find.

The Emergency Response Manager has called a teleconference meeting for the Senior Team and the TPP 'en route' to the CMC. This is to determine the facts and activate the Go Team.

On arrival at the CMC, the Operations Manager is the first to arrive as she only lives ten minutes away. What are the first tasks she must do to ensure the CMC is operational as soon as possible?

What information can she put on the whiteboard to start populating it at this early stage?

Notes

1 NTSB – National Transportation Safety Board – US investigation department used for all transport incidents and accidents with a worldwide reputation. They are usually called upon for air accidents internationally.
2 FAA – Federal Aviation Administration – US-based agency that controls the aviation in, out and over US airspace. Regulates policies on safety and security within US aviation.
3 CAA – Civil Aviation Authority – UK-based agency that controls aviation in, out and over UK airspace. Regulates policies on safety and security within UK aviation.
4 AAIB – Air Accident Investigation Branch – UK-led Government department that specialises in air accidents.
5 Different regions of the world may have specific requirements on timescales.
6 Dark Site – disabling some of the interactive aspects or hiding specific pages of a website, even if temporarily (also see Chapter 8).
7 NTSB final report on Asiana 214 – www.ntsb.gov/investigations/accidentreports/reports/aar1401.pdf.

References and Additional Reading

Cilliers, P. (1998). *Complexity and Postmodernism: Understanding Complex Systems*. London: Routledge.
Coombs, W. T., & Holliday, S. J. (2004). Unpacking the Halo Effect: Reputation and Crisis Management. *Journal of Communication Management*, 10 (2) pp. 123–137. https://doi.org/10.1108/13632540610664698.
Family Assistance Act. (1996/2000). (Online). Available at: www.ntsb.gov/tda/er/Pages/tda-fa-aviation.aspx.
Harris, A. (2004). Lifeline: Call Centers and Crisis Management. *Risk Management*, 55 (5) pp. 42–45, 8.
ICAO. (2013a). *Assistance to Aircraft Accident Victims and Families, Doc 9998/499*. Montreal: International Civil Aviation Organization.
ICAO. (2013b). *Assistance to Aircraft Accident Victims and Families, 9973/486*. Montreal: International Civil Aviation Organization.
ICAO. (2021). *Annex 13 to the Convention on International Civil Aviation Organization: 12th Ed. Aircraft Accident and Incident Investigation*. Montreal: International Civil Aviation Organization.
International Criminal Police Organisation (INTERPOL). (2019). *Guide to Disaster Victim Identification*. (Online). Available at: www.interpol.int/en.
Teleworldwire.com. (2022). *Florida Division of Emergency Management Deploys Contact Centre to Serve Residents Impacted by Hurricane Ian*. (Online). Available at: www.proquest.com/trade-journals/florida-division-emergency-management-deploys/docview/2726429603/se-2?accountid=7179.
Venugopal, S., Li, H., & Ray, P. (2011). Auto-Scaling Emergency Call Centres Using Cloud Resources to Handle Disasters. *2011 IEEE Nineteenth IEEE International Workshop on Quality of Service*, San Jose, CA, USA, pp. 1–9. https://doi.org/10.1109/IWQOS.2011.5931344.

4 Airline Go Teams

Chapter Objectives

By the end of this chapter, you will be able to:

- Explain what an airline Go Team is and what they do when activated
- Understand who is suitable to be part of an airline Go Team
- Describe the range of roles in a Go Team
- Understand and explain the first actions of the Go Team on arrival
- Explain who the Go Team report to on arrival, and why?

Opening Quiz

1. What do you understand an airline Go Team is?
2. What are the key tasks and actions for a Go Team?
3. What skills and capabilities make a good Go Team member?
4. Why does an airline need a Go Team?
5. What other agencies in aviation response would also have Go Teams?

Glossary for this Chapter

CMC   Crisis Management Centre
FAA   Federal Aviation Authority
HAC   Humanitarian Assistance Centre
NTSB   National Transportation Safety Bureau

Chapter Introduction

According to the NTSB, a Go Team

> consists of technical experts needed to solve complex transportation safety problems. Specialists across the agency have a rotational duty assignment to respond as quickly as possible to the scene of the accident. Go Teams travel by commercial airliner or government aircraft depending on circumstances and availability.
>
> (NTSB, 2023)

DOI: 10.4324/9781003405337-7

So, an aviation Go Team needs to be made up of a wide range of skills and roles and available to be deployed in the first phases of a response when there may be little in the way of infrastructure and services to support them. In terms of the Crisis Management Centre (CMC) activation process, these are the personnel that should be called first to put on standby and get ready to leave at short notice. All members of the Go Team should have a personal '*go kit*' ready to adapt to whatever climate and location they are deployed to, which is detailed later on in the chapter.

Initial Role of the Go Team

Once activated, the Go Team becomes the '*eyes and ears*' of the airline via the CMC. They may have to travel to the location by way of a range of routes if the location is challenging to reach or by military aircraft if required.

Go Teams can take many forms. The NTSB version of a Go Team is very much based on an investigatory team, which is logical, but from an airlines' perspective, a Go Team really needs to be a mixed team of skills and roles to offer the best spread of experience to support the teams at the site and to aid the authorities during an investigation.

A mix of skills could include any of the following as appropriate at the time of activation: engineers, flight deck, crew management, HR, logistics, admin support, legal, finance, senior managers, security, IT and operations staff. Each type of organisation involved in an accident will have its own Go Team, so it is best to concentrate on just airlines for the purposes of this chapter.

Recruitment and activation of this crucial team will be central to any airline plans and emergency strategy. They need to be well trained and exercised so, to an extent, they understand what to expect and what to do on arrival. Unless they have a background in the military (for example), this can be challenging to achieve. But in any case, they should have an investment of time and training so they can understand the complexity and demands of being a Go Team member.

Another key recruitment point to consider is the requirement to activate anywhere in the world at short notice. This might require some thought and support put in place by airlines to enable this to happen, given lifestyles, caring responsibilities and roles within the organisation, but essentially, not being able to activate and deploy without notice may be a barrier to inclusion as part of the team. Clearly, at the time of activation, not everyone may be able to activate due to illness, etc., so having enough Go Team members in place is a sensible contingency. Not sending a Go Team is not acceptable and is a requirement of the Family Assistance Act (1996/2000).

 Tip

When recruiting for a Go Team, it might be useful to undertake an airline audit of skills, languages, previous experience, etc. Often, those individuals who have experience in the military, police, paramedics, volunteer mountain rescue, etc., can make good Go Team members as they can work under pressure and have experience working in these types of situations. Of course, these things are always voluntary (unless it's specifically part of the role), but knowing who in advance and making the team up of those that can work well if trained supports a solid airline response plan.

How to Train a Go Team

Once recruited, and this might be via volunteering or by role, i.e., engineering or senior manager, etc., then ensuring the Go Team are fully aware of their role and are trained for it is essential. As Figure 4.1 details a Go Team should be made up of a diverse team of skills and experience from within the airline.

Often, airlines do not have the '*field*' experience to undertake this and bring in an outside source to do this part for them, such as a Third Party Provider (TPP). The TPP can supplement an airline Go Team as the teams need to have a fully immersive training experience to undertake what they might see and experience as the first airline personnel at the scene of an accident (Kann & Draper, 2013).

Training elements should include:

1. Understanding what their role is during deployment as it might be different from their normal commercial role. An example might be operations staff in planning, and rosters might be part of the Go Team
2. The expectations of the airline for behaviour and boundaries once at the incident site. Who can they talk to and who should they make contact with, etc.?
3. Preparing them for the experience of walking into an accident situation either at the crash site or within a Humanitarian Assistance Centre (HAC) and knowing they are representing the airline in a very visual way. This can be challenging for many people, and Go Team members should be prepared fully for this (Jehn & Techakesari, 2014).
4. How to activate and the process and procedures for deployment, e.g., where to go? What to take? What vaccinations and visas may be required for entry into the country?

First Priorities on the Ground

Once activated and deployed to the location, the first priorities of the Go Team are to make contact with the authorities to let them know they are there as the airline's representatives and where they can be found for support, e.g., a hotel or an HAC if already set up. This can be a lengthy process as, often, local authorities do not always want to have contact initially with the airline

Figure 4.1 Types of roles that can make up an airline Go Team

which may be at the centre of a major accident. It can take patience and time for authorities and investigating teams to reach out to airline Go Teams after the initial phase of securing the site and starting the investigation. This support is detailed in the Family Assistance Act (1996/2000), showing that the airline is part of the support process. While waiting for the authorities or investigating teams to contact them, they undertake other actions like situating themselves at the airport, relieving staff who may have been on duty for many hours and working with the CMC to understand the local situation.

In aviation, the first location that a Go Team will go to on arrival is the airport where the aircraft took off from or was supposed to land. For MH17,[1] the Go Team was sent to Amsterdam airport in order to take over from the check-in staff who had been '*managing*' the crisis since it happened. There is often a vacuum for airline staff who must be able to '*manage*' accidents until the Go Teams arrive. This can be traumatic for these teams who may or may not have had training and experience for this, and the importance of a stable and well-trained Go Team comes into its own here. They were able to stand down the staff who had been on duty for 24 hours and who had '*dispatched*' the flight so that they could rest and response procedures could be escalated.

Once the contacts have been made, local staff relieved, and an initial report made to the CMC on conditions and the situation, the next challenge for the Go Team is to establish contact with the relevant embassies. This can be determined from the passenger manifest list. Of course, this may not always be 100% accurate in terms of nationality as passengers can possess several passports, but at least starting the contact process can determine this information.

The Go Team needs an office, and this might be at the airline offices if it is near to the accident site. If, however, the site is not in the vicinity of an office or in a location where there are no airline offices, then establishing a location at the airport or a nearby hotel is essential. Starting a logbook as per the crisis management process is vital for retaining information that could be used later during an inquiry, etc.

Contact back at the CMC should be regular as the Go Team are the '*eyes and ears*' of the CMC team at the site. Buying local phones with local SIM cards can be beneficial to prevent personal phones from having to be used, but company phones may be useful at this time.

Clearly, the Go Team often deploys without the full picture being established, and this level of ambiguity is normal. Being flexible and able to work with ambiguity is really a core characteristic needed for Go Team members. Often, Go Teams arrive at a destination with no accommodation, no office and no contact and it is their job to build these early infrastructure elements before the bulk of the airline responders arrive. Being able to make quick decisions on little or no information available is crucial, but so is making decisions in a calm and objective way. Therefore, contact with the CMC, wherever possible, is essential as the team in the CMC may have additional information that can offer direction to the team.

Once the essentials are established, then accommodation must be sought. If a HAC has been secured by the CMC and is ready for the families and airline responders, the Go Team should be included in the figures needed for accommodation. However, this may not be possible during the first day of the arrival, so accommodation can be challenging.

Along with accommodation is the need to buy food and secure transport. Having access to company funds through a company credit card can be essential, but also having cash in the form of dollars (usually) is also a helpful starting point for arrival, especially if the location requires cash-led transactions.[2] To secure hotels for HACs and accommodation, transport for potentially large numbers of people and feeding them 24/7 can be an expensive operation and can often only be secured at the location. Therefore, Finance needs to represented in the Go Team to ensure access to company funds.

Please note that the insurance company that is underwriting the accident operations pays for accommodation, etc., but in the beginning of an event, the contract will take time to be activated. Airlines are expected to pay upfront for services they will need to establish the support stated in the Family Assistance Act (1996/2000) and ICAO requirements. This is not an insubstantial amount of funds required. Even the leanest of airlines must have a fund available for just such an occasion, and having immediate access to it for the Go Team is required to pay for what is required.

Once established with an office, access to WIFI, mobiles, food, etc., reporting to the governmental offices of embassies, investigation teams and airline offices in the location, they will be given specific tasks or actions to complete that will vary from accident to accident.

Go Team Kit

The following is a suggested list of clothing and personal equipment that airline Go Teams should have in the event of being deployed.

Suggested Personal Go Team Kit

The list in Table 4.1 was put together with the aid of an experienced Go Team member and is not an exhaustive list.

Some countries prohibit the importation of various items, including some foods, meats, dairy products, weapons and bladed articles (possibly including those carried for cultural or religious reasons), prescription medication and other over-the-counter medicines.

Some countries also question the requirement for expensive or specialist photographic equipment fitted with additional lenses used by Go Teams for photographing the crash site and evidence as part of their role in assisting the investigating teams (the possible intimation will be involvement in espionage, etc.).

Table 4.1 List of Go Team personal considerations for a deployment

Bag/suitcase for personal belongings	Plain if possible	Be aware there may be media representatives at the airport/port of arrival/hotel seeking to identify responders for news outlets and to obtain information
		Any outside luggage labels should not have company references/logos
Day bag	For everyday use	Plain if possible – a rucksack type bag is an example
		Any outside luggage labels should not have company references/logos
Papers	Passport (with minimum six months validity from **date of issue**)	Spare passport photos and copies of your passport (it is also suggested you have a photo of your passport on your phone)
		Some airlines issue Go Teams with two passports, one for normal operational travel and one specifically for deployment to keep it *'clean'* of potentially controversial stamps
	Visa(s) if required	Cash for arrival and exit visas, as many have to be paid in cash – check with the office BEFORE travel
	Covid Vaccination Certificates	Any specific PCR Tests/other tests/Passenger Locator Forms, etc., as required
	Vaccination Certificates	A current record of vaccinations and boosters if applicable

(Continued)

Table 1.4 (Continued)

Shoes	Work	Off duty
Boots/sturdy footwear	Work	Health and Safety – if additional specialist footwear is required, this will be provided
Trousers/skirts/dresses	Work	Off duty
Shirts/blouses	Work	Off duty
Polo shirts/T shirts	Work	Off duty
Hat	Warm Weather	Cold Weather
Scarf/head scarf	For respectful cultural/ religious compliance. Some cultures require heads/hair to be covered	Please try to avoid the colour red as this has a number of different meanings in different cultures
Gloves		Cold weather
Coat	Wet/cold weather	Consider a lightweight jacket should the temperature in a warm environment drop of an evening
Tie (Male)	Dark and light colour	Please try to avoid the colour red as this has a number of different meanings in different cultures
Shorts/gym/exercise clothing		For when off duty and if the opportunity arises and it is permitted culturally
Clothing for memorials/official visits and occasions	Suit/smart casual or similar – for formal occasions	Sometimes, Go Teams may be required to attend a local memorial service, funeral, cremation or other form of service Additionally, they may have to attend official premises, including embassies and other official buildings, meetings or functions
Wash kit/cosmetics	Personal grooming, hygiene and cosmetics requirements, sufficient for a minimum of two weeks (Remember the size restrictions if carried in hand luggage on aircraft)	This includes any electrical equipment such as shavers and hairdryers, don't forget to pack an appropriate travel adapter
Night attire/sleepwear	As required	Sleeping conditions may be very basic
Medications (prescribed)	Sufficient for a minimum of two weeks – it may not be possible to obtain prescribed medication overseas	Prescribed medication should be in the original packaging and, if possible, un-opened. It is advisable to have a copy of the prescription or a list of prescribed medication; this can assist if questioned at customs, also a letter from a Doctor and contact details for the prescribing Doctor and pharmacy)
Medications (non-prescribed)		Medication should be in the original packaging and, if possible unopened Some countries prohibit the importation of medications that can be bought over the counter in the UK/US (for example) to treat conditions such as diarrhoea/vomiting or pain relief – check prior to travel

As this list shows, it is comprehensive to ensure Go Teams are self-sufficient and do not (as much as possible) impact the local infrastructure. The list also shows that it would be difficult to put this together with 30 minutes' notice (for example), and having a partially packed kit for personal use is recommended by the NTSB.

Other non-essential considerations for Go Team members can include:

- Clothes washing powder/liquid (for hand washing of clothes, depending on the location)
- Ear plugs – to assist sleeping
- Electrical travel plugs/adapters
- Headphones/earbuds
- Laptops/tablet with cables and chargers
- List of emergency contacts (ICE – In case of emergency)
- Local currency, if available
- Notebook
- Pens
- Phone with cables and charger (check supplier roaming charges if the phone is a personal one)
- Spare spectacles (if worn) or contact lenses
- Sunglasses
- Tissues – for personal hygiene
- Water bottle (so it can be refilled)

Ongoing Role of the Go Team

Once the initial phase of the response has moved to the '*accident site management*' phase, the Go Team can focus on their more specialist skills and expertise.

Working closely with the investigation teams and HAC teams, the Go Team usually turns to more focused tasks and actions such as supporting the '*search and recovery*' teams (see Chapter 10).

The work of the Go Team is completely flexible and can change from day to day. Often due to specific skills such as identification, repatriation or personal effects, they can transfer to other teams as the Go Team duties decrease and other teams arrive to take over key roles, i.e., search and recovery and SAT members.

The Go Team could rotate out of the operation and come back to the CMC if their work is complete once the operation increases elsewhere. The decision on how to use the Go Team at this point would be decided by the CMC.

Conclusions

The Go Teams are a trusted and well-trained group of individuals who have a range of skills and experience that deploy on behalf of the airline to the accident site. They are flexible and are the '*eyes and ears*' of the management teams in the CMC to gather vital situational information to support operational decisions. They then can transfer out of the Go Team into other vital specialisms depending on their experience and skills or transfer home.

They must be independent, able to '*think on their feet*', be able to be comfortable with sleeping in less than luxurious conditions, depending on the location and severity of the accident, and be able to offer calm and considered information to the CMC.

Key Points from this Chapter

- The Go Team can be made up of a range of skills and roles depending on their experience and the situation at the time
- They report back to the CMC to give up-to-date reports on the situation and the challenges locally
- The Go Team will make contact with the embassies, investigating teams, authorities and other agencies when they arrive to offer support and assistance to them
- The Go Teams need to be able to deploy immediately and be self-sufficient for approx. two weeks by means of their own personal kits
- Once contact has been established, and other airline teams start to arrive, the Go Teams can transition to other specialist teams or come back to the CMC

Quiz

Take a few minutes to complete this quiz to check your understanding of this chapter.

1. What type of roles or skills is the Go Team made up of?
2. Why does the CMC send a Go Team initially to the accident location?
3. What are three of the initial tasks the Go Team can be asked to undertake on arrival?
4. Why is training so important for a Go Team?
5. Name three things that the Go team needs in their kit.

Notes

1 MH17 – Malaysian airlines from Amsterdam to Kuala Lumpur was shot down in Ukraine in July 2014.
2 Cash-led transactions – Some regions may not have ATMs or prefer use of cash so Go Teams may sometimes have to carry significant amounts of cash to secure accommodation, transport and food initially. Most countries will accept US dollars.

References and Additional Reading

Family Assistance Act. (1996/2000). (Online). Available at: www.ntsb.gov/tda/er/Pages/tda-fa-aviation. aspx.

Jehn, K. A., & Techakesari, P. (2014). High Reliability Teams: New Directions for Disaster Management and Conflict. *International Journal of Conflict Management*, 25 (4) pp. 407–430. https://doi.org/10.1108/IJCMA-02–2014–0019.

Kann, D. F., & Draper, T. W. (2013). Plane Down in the City: Operation Crash and Surge. *Journal of Business Continuity & Emergency Planning*, 7 (3) pp. 184–192.

NTSB. (2023). *Go Teams*. (Online). Available at: www.ntsb.gov/investigations/process/Pages/goteam. aspx.

5 Airline Special Assistance Teams (SAT)

Chapter Objectives

By the end of this chapter, you will be able to:

- Explain what a Special Assistance Team (SAT) is and what their role is during a deployment
- Describe the various locations where the SATs support families and survivors of accidents
- List some of the tasks and actions for a SAT whilst at the Humanitarian Assistance Centre (HAC)
- Explain some of the boundaries put in place to protect SATs

Opening Quiz

1. What is an airline SAT?
2. What is their role in an accident?
3. Where will they usually be based?
4. Where else can they be based?
5. Why do airlines have to send SATs to the HAC to support survivors and families?

Glossary for this chapter

DVI Disaster Victim Identification. Forensic teams that support the identification of individuals from aviation disasters.
HAC Humanitarian Assistance Centre
HR Human Resources
IMC Incident Management Centre
SAT Special Assistance Teams
TPP Third-Party Providers

Note – Facebook® is now called Meta®

Chapter Introduction

Special Assistance Teams (or Team members) are a group of trained volunteers from within the airline that activate and deploy when required to support the airline passengers, crew and members of the public in times of crisis. This can include everything from weather disruption to

DOI: 10.4324/9781003405337-8

full airline disasters. An example to illustrate this could be the wildfires in Greece in 2023 when several UK-based airlines sent out SATs on board empty aircraft to support their customers and help bring the stranded passengers home.

Usually taken from a variety of roles within the airline, from cabin crew to ground staff, they deploy as representatives of the airline who can support those impacted by the airline accident. It is a requirement under the Family Assistance Act (1996/2000) that airlines must have a trained team of SAT members who can support those impacted by an accident.

The other term these teams can be known by is *'Care Teams'*. Some airlines use this term for their SAT teams, but they are the same thing. The preference is down to each airline.[1]

The reality of the situation is, however, that most airlines would not have enough personnel to deploy for a large-scale disaster and are usually supplemented by TPP's who have large numbers of skilled and well-trained individuals who can support the airline SATs at the HAC. This is, of course, if the airline has a contract to retain this service.

The normal calculation in terms of the airline insurance agreements for those who attend the HAC is an approximate figure of four people per person named on the manifest, regardless of whether injured or deceased. This means that for a standard Boeing 737MAX, it would be approximately 200 passengers, giving a rough figure of potentially 800 people to accommodate and support at the HAC. Clearly, there are only one or two airlines in the world big enough to have an internal team of SATs to undertake this without external help.

The reality of the situation is nowhere near that many come to the HAC as most tend to stay at home due to technological advances in communication, but even if only 50% arrive, then that could be 400 people to accommodate and support. That means that SATs have to be recruited, trained and ready to activate and deploy, and this is a huge requirement for the airline to undertake.

Recruiting Special Assistance Teams

Recruiting SATs can be quite challenging for a variety of reasons. Turnover of staff and seasonal staff mean the turnaround of new SAT members can be constant. Also, the requirement to be able to activate and deploy at short notice for anything up to two weeks at a time for the worst-case scenarios may well be a barrier for those volunteers who have caring responsibilities or roles that are deemed *'essential'* to the operation. That said, understanding you have rotations of SATs at an HAC if the centre is open for longer than a couple of weeks, being a carer would not preclude anyone from being a SAT member as they could go on a subsequent rotation given the time to organise and manage their responsibilities.

Recruitment can take many forms. Either on a volunteer basis, where most SATs come from, or linked to a specific role. That, however, can be much more problematic if the individual does not especially care for being on an SAT as it may overwhelm and, in some extreme cases, traumatise them. It is always better to have volunteer SAT members.

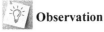 **Observation**

If you look at your total number of employees and also the requirement to run an airline operation alongside an accident, your ability to deploy a team of SATs as well as a Go Team to an HAC, set it up and run it means you would probably need far more staff than you already have. If you have a contract with a TPP, check to see if the service for SATs is included. Then work with them to build a good relationship so the two parties train together and exercise together before you might need them.

Honesty is key to recruiting good SATs. Remember, these people represent the airline and the brand and support highly traumatised people impacted directly by the airline. It is not an easy role to fulfil. Being truthful about the role will help those who volunteer to understand the enormity of the responsibilities they may have to face.

Be aware of triggers for staff. The airline might have really well-intentioned staff who want to be SATs but might have a personal trauma that, if they deployed, may be triggered. Being honest and exploring all these issues at the beginning is far better than having to send home a SAT who has been triggered by the accident they are supporting and may well need much more intervention when at home again (Quevillon, Gray, Erikson & Jacobs, 2016). Some airlines employ psychologists to pre-screen volunteers before training.

Table 5.1 offers a range of skills and capabilities that good SATs will be able to offer for the role. Clearly, each accident and situation is different and may need specific skills, but this shows the range and variety when recruiting.

Training Special Assistance Teams

SATs, just like Go Teams, need training and exercises to keep them current and able to deploy confidently. Initial training undertaken by skilled and experienced personnel is essential to offer the SATs the full picture of what to expect. Giving everyone a '*get out option*' after the training is also necessary. Being really honest about what they might witness, experience and feel whilst on deployment and also the long-term impact it can have on them, be it positive or negative, is key to being left with a team of people who are fully aware of what they are getting into and are prepared for.

As discussed earlier, having a mix of experienced SATs from the TPP and the airline can work well. TPPs have experienced people who can spot those in distress quickly, support airline SATs who may be new to the role and help to mentor and coach first-hand. The most '*successful*' accident operations have been those where the airline and the TPP have worked together before needing to deploy and have worked together on deployment in a harmonious way. Using scenarios or case studies can be a good starting point for training as they can be '*frozen*' and

Table 5.1 The core range of skills needed by a SAT member

Skill Required	Skill Used	Potential Issues
Languages	Translation	Need to translate terrible news or details to families about their loved ones
Cultural experience	Advice for CMC/IMC and HAC on how to ensure cultural compassion	Can be caught up in cultural nuance, i.e., how death rituals are completed
Prior experience of this type of work	Used for training, mentoring and guidance at the HAC	Might find being a SAT triggering
Flexible	Quick change roles and requirements	Can be a challenging and frustrating role if not truly flexible, as tasks and deadlines change dynamically
Assertive, but not aggressive	Able to support families but understand boundaries	Being able to say '*no*' to demands of someone, even if the request is unreasonable, can be upsetting
Good listener	For traumatised people to talk to (NOT counsel)	Can find themselves taking on too much trauma
People-centred individual	Need to care about people	Can find themselves taking on too much trauma

discussed without putting the training SAT members under undue pressure. Allowing for an element of media interaction is also useful to prepare those who will deploy for how to communicate with the media (Rowntree & Akerlund, 2012).

As Table 5.1 illustrates, for every skill, there can be a potential issue. A good example is using people's language capabilities at the HAC to translate for families and/or investigating teams. The need to tell the families their loved one has been positively identified or retelling details from the investigation teams to a family question at a daily briefing can be a challenge to the resilience of the individual. Another example might be that being a good listener means a family member may tell the SAT lots of personal and graphic details about their relationship with their loved one that the SAT member will need to keep confidential. This can be hard for an individual to do if they have no previous counselling training.

It is important during training for SATs that they fully understand that SAT members are not counsellors. Even if they have experience and qualifications in that area, it is not appropriate as part of the role. The role of the SAT is very clear in all requirements set out by ICAO and the Family Assistance Act (1996/2000). It is a practical and professional role to support the initial needs of those who attend the HAC. SAT members can get very close to the families they support, and there is a danger of becoming a '*pseudo counsellor*'. During training, it is vital that SAT members understand what their role entails and where their role ends.

Activation and Deployment

Activation for SATs would be initiated from the CMC in the form of sending out an SMS message asking who would be available to deploy (see Chapter 3 for details). The role of the team in the CMC after receiving back responses would be to gather an initial SAT that could deploy straight away and record those who might need to be on a second rotation. Putting the first group on standby is essential until enough information is understood about the situation before deploying them to the location. This is slightly different than the Go Team, which the CMC would usually deploy straight away with little information to ascertain the situation '*on the ground*'. As the HAC needs to be up and running within the first 24 hours (as per the Family Assistance Act, 1996/2000), taking a little time to ensure the location of the HAC, book accommodation for a SAT that may, in the worst case scenario, be sizable (potentially 100+) and how they will be transported to the location is essential. Another consideration would be the safety of the SAT, depending on the geopolitics and location of the accident. Finally, deciding how many airline SAT members and how many TPP SAT members to send as a combined team will depend on information about the numbers concerned and how many SAT members reply to the initial SMS.

Once a number is agreed for deployment to a specific location to work in a named HAC, then the team can be sent to the location with a clearly defined structure for management, either from within the airline or to meet up with the TPP SAT members, who may well be there first and setting up the HAC.

Airlines can sometimes have a '*SAT Go Team*' made up of experienced and well-trained individuals who may have deployed before or who have previous experience, i.e., military or police, and they can deploy with the Go team to specifically set up an HAC and help the airport that might be accommodating families or survivors. This is not usual, and often happens for larger airlines.

Initially, asking for help from an alliance partner or a codeshare partner can fill a potential vacuum as the airline SAT deploys to the location. This is especially helpful for languages and help at an airport for families.[2]

Figure 5.1 Three phases of deploying an airline SAT

Agreeing on how long SATs can stay and their role once at the HAC means the team in the CMC, with the overall management of the SAT can start to plan the rotations moving forward using those individuals who responded with '*maybe*' but are unable to deploy straight away. Figure 5.1 illustrates the three key phases of deployment from phase one (1–12 hours), phase two (within five to seven days) and phase three (within 14 days). Having an idea about who can deploy and when allows for airlines, especially HR departments, to plan a roster period, usually for the first two weeks in three phases.

This means an airline can rotate a new support SAT out to the HAC over the first 14 days when a decision can be made on the size of the operation. It is always best to send more at the beginning of an operation and be in a position to be able to release SAT members earlier to come home than not send enough.

One sizable question for airlines to agree on is whether the airline SAT wears uniforms or not. It is usual for a SAT to wear casual office attire to perform their duties as wearing uniforms can make them a target for the media and other passengers and may form an '*invisible*' barrier with the families they are there to support. Often, wearing a uniform simply '*gets in the way*' of the role they are there to perform. If asked by the families, it is perfectly acceptable and, in fact, crucial both the airline and TPP SAT members are honest about the fact that they work for the airline, but it may not be advisable to advertise the fact by means of a clearly identifiable uniform. This can also lead to extra media scrutiny as those wearing uniforms are clearly visible to journalists.

Accommodation may be basic if away from the HAC as, clearly, it is unlikely that hotels can take families and SAT members as well as Disaster Victim Identification (DVI) teams, authorities and management in one location. Airline SATs need to be prepared to work and sleep in different locations. Being a SAT member requires flexibility and stamina. The days are long; SAT members will be on their feet a great deal, and they might have to travel 30+ minutes at the end of a long shift to their accommodation that might not be luxurious. This means if staying at a five-star hotel, with a minimum level of luxury is a requirement to deploy, the role may not be suitable. Being honest during the training phase can eliminate those individuals who may not be able to undertake the complexities of the role.

Locations for Special Assistance Team Members

SAT members can be utilised in three main locations. In the HAC, to support travelling families and survivors. Secondly, at the hospitals accommodating the injured survivors, and lastly, in family's homes of those who cannot, or do not want to, travel to the HAC. For planning purposes airlines may need to deploy personnel to more than one location and Table 5.2 shows the three main locations for SAT members to be sent initially.

Other destinations that an SAT member could be deployed to are the crew HAC, if this is relevant and/or the Survivors HAC, again if relevant. Sometimes, these groups have different HACs but with the same level of service and support given by the teams. (See Chapter 7 for more detail).

Table 5.2 Three main locations for SAT members

Location	Key Points	Potential Issues
HAC	To support a 24/7 operation taking care of multiple families	Initially, it could be hundreds but then quickly scaled down as the HAC reduces in families over the weeks
Hospitals	To support the injured. Usually not at the bedside, but that is location-dependent	Can be refused access by the hospital, especially if the injuries are severe. Can involve long hours of waiting with little to do. Needs to be two SATs per patient for duty of care and mutual support
Homes	Supporting families in their own homes by staying nearby and reporting to the homes daily to update on new information and support	Can be refused access by the families. Sometimes, can be met with initial aggression until trust is made. There needs to be at least two SATs for duty of care and mutual support

Humanitarian Assistance Centre

SATs will arrive at the HAC and prepare it for opening. According to ICAO Annex 13 and the Family Assistance Act (1996/2000), the HAC needs to be open and ready to receive families within the first 24 hours. The reality is because the airport wants to transfer families and survivors to the HAC as soon as possible, SATs can arrive with families already waiting for them.

By sending out experienced teams first and utilising the TPP Go Team, this can be accommodated, and set up can be, and usually is, much quicker than the 24 hours proposed.

Initially, the equipment sent out with the SATs can help the team be self-sufficient for 48 hours and expedite the setting up of the HAC. This would include:

- Paper, files, manuals and stationery
- Mobile phones for use with local SIMs
- Items used for the multi-faith room
- Items used for the childcare rooms
- Items to set up the incident management centre (IMC) office

See Chapter 7, HAC Management, for more details on separate areas in the HAC to which this list relates.

Overview of Daily Tasks for a Special Assistance Team Member Working in a Humanitarian Assistance Centre

Each day can be different, and definitely each deployment is different in terms of numbers involved, cultures, languages, religions and demographics, but there are some themes that run through each accident, and that is what the SAT members do each day they are on duty at the HAC.

SATs are given a manual on arrival that might have checklists in, things to remember and a note-taking section. The idea is that SAT members should write down where they have been and for how long, who with, the meetings they attend and who else was there. These are considered vital information for a later inquiry and evidence of the support offered at the HAC by the airline through the SATs.[3]

Mornings are usually the busiest. This is due to the daily briefings held each day, or multiple times each day, depending on the situation, and for meetings with authorities for the families.

The daily briefings are held for a variety of reasons. This is the one way that the investigation teams, agencies involved in search and recovery, DVI teams, Government departments and the airline can update the families and survivors.

The daily briefing can only happen once, so there cannot be *'shifts'* of sessions. This means the HAC needs to have a conference room big enough to accommodate everyone in one go, or a supplementary location would be needed, such as a conference centre that could. If using a conference centre, then the families, survivors and all relevant parties would need to be transported there and back. It also has the added challenge of security and keeping the media out (for specific layouts for daily briefings, see Chapter 7).

Having a briefing within the hotel is always the preferred option as it is easier to ensure the rooms are secure and can be kept private to allow everyone attending to hear the information, updates and reports from the presenters **BEFORE** it is released to the media. This does not always work as the information can be leaked from within the room, as families and survivors may want to record the proceedings or upload it to their social media sites. This is allowed but discouraged until after the authorities have presented to the key people first.

The family briefing takes place at the same time each day. Usually between 0800–0900 local time and then if a second one is required in the evening. The setup is also kept consistent so that the room is set up for translation services. This is either via headsets and a live translator in the room or by a *'conferencing kit'* that automatically translates if a live translator cannot be sourced or the numbers require a certain language.[4]

The room also has speaker systems and microphones to allow everyone to hear what is being said and to accommodate questions from the floor to the presenters. The presenters often sit at the far end of the room so that they can use any technical equipment, i.e., slides or videos, as appropriate.

The briefing usually takes around one hour, depending on the information and updates. At this time, SAT members will not be in the room unless asked to be there by the family they are supporting and, of course, if numbers allow.

Meetings with authorities could include the Coroner (Medical Examiner in the US), police authorities, investigating teams, and any other agency that potentially require information from the family as part of the identification or investigation process or for the families to ask whatever questions they might have about their loved ones or the investigation. Figure 5.2 indicates the range of participants that may wish to be in attendance at the family briefing. The SAT member will accompany the families to the meetings, ensuring transport is booked and anything they might need is available to them as part of their role as practical support.

Ante-mortem meetings usually take place in the afternoon at the HAC and are more complex and involve asking questions of the families about their loved ones that can help the mortuary teams positively identify them. This could be physical features, clothing, piercings or any other distinctive feature that could support the post-mortem information. Ante-mortem forms come from INTERPOL (see Chapter 7 for details).

Professional Boundaries

As part of the training process, giving clear professional boundaries for SAT members is crucial to minimise potential issues post-deployment. Understanding their role as the airline representative offering support at the HAC and not as a *'best friend'*, being professional, empathetic and flexible. Also, knowing when to step back or away from situations, when to seek help and when to walk away at the end of their rotation.

Being a professional SAT is really core for a successful deployment. The families that the SAT may be supporting can be traumatised, angry, dysfunctional or toxic, just like before the

Figure 5.2 Who may participate in a family briefing?

accident. All families are different, and how they relate to each other in terms of behaviours, emotions and conflict is also different. The role of the SAT is not to play referee to family disputes played out at the HAC but to have a small but significant distance from the families so they are available to practically support them, arrange transport to Coroners' offices, be in the room when a positive identification of their loved one is given, be available if personal effects are returned and listen to them when they want to talk about their loved one, but as a professional person not as an additional family member. This is incredibly demanding to do and do well, but doing it well is a must if the SAT member wants to avoid being dragged into situations that they need not be part of and potentially make situations worse. An example could be a long-running family dispute when siblings have not seen each other or spoken in years but are brought together due to the death of a parent. They may not feel able to set aside their dispute, but the SAT member must not allow themselves to be dragged in and remain objective.

Not going to family rooms or exchanging phone numbers is also a boundary well worth emphasising. Again, a slight distance, this time physically, to ensure that all interactions take place within the structure of the HAC, not alone in a hotel room, is a *'duty of care'* that keeps both sides safe.

Not exchanging addresses and phone numbers is an important boundary to clarify. This may seem petty given the experience of the families at the HAC, but the relationship is short-term and defined. It exists between the airline and the family, not the individual as such. Once the SAT member leaves the HAC, the relationship remains with the airline but with a different SAT member if rotating into the HAC. If the relationship exists outside the HAC, the psychological line has been crossed whereby the SAT member may be a reminder of the traumatic experience in the HAC and become part of the problem of triggering for the family. Explaining this clearly with honesty and examples during training will help to minimise this issue.

For TPPs, stepping over the agreed boundaries of keeping a professional distance, not going to family's rooms, exchanging contact details or seeing the families they support after deployment is taken very seriously and is usually deemed to be an offence that means the individual would never be deployed again. For airlines, the line is more blurred given the potentially longer-term relationship between the families and the airline, but understanding that they are there to support the families but not become part of the family they support is a distinction worth taking seriously to avoid situations that may impact negatively on an individual or airline brand reputation.

Case Study 4 – Interview with an Experienced Special Assistance Team Manager

Note the interviewee deployed on behalf of a national airline.

The individual interviewed is an experienced SAT Manager. Having worked for a national airline and then more recently by deploying for a TPP, they have deployed to some of the most high-profile airline accidents and were able to offer their perspective on the reality of the role. They deployed to two accidents in quick succession and were able to compare the experience of them both.

What do you see as your role as an SAT member?

Essentially, that it's providing support, care and *'assistance'*. What this means is it can be handing out the hanky, it can be a cup of tea, it can be anything that anyone under duress might require. So, it's really an open book. If I had to write a manual on exactly what an SAT does, I couldn't. It's so varied and open about what you end up doing. We also use the term Care Team as that's what we do. We care for people at the HAC.

It also takes a certain kind of character or personality to be able to be on this team and to be able to deliver well. You know they lead from the heart more than perhaps always being logical. You are there to help people who are under enormous stress in a high-pressure environment.

How did the training you received link to your real experience?

Training is good. Training helps. Manuals are good. They also help. It sets the stage. It gives you an overarching view. It gives you the ideals of which you need to work in that situation. But did it actually set me up for the deployments I then went to? Not entirely. On the flip side, would I have been able to endure and go through those deployments without the training? Probably not. So, the training helps, but there will never ever be a training or a manual that is entirely comprehensive, and there never could be.

What do you see as the most important skills needed for a SAT?

Multitasking, thinking on your feet and having personal resilience. Not having to rely on manuals, so you need to be well-read or well-versed with the role, but more importantly, know that understanding what to do in theory is not good enough. That's just knowledge. The wisdom comes in when you get there. Just because you might have an emergency role in the airline doesn't automatically mean you can deal with it when it actually happens. Because you can't guarantee that the person who has that role has the ability to then switch to an emergency, which we all know is over and above our everyday jobs.

Another thing is the ability to leave a role at the door. Even if you are a senior person in the airline, at an HAC the SAT members need to leave role, rank and ego at the door to be able to work together as a cohesive team. You need empathy and a desire to serve people.

You've mentioned resilience; what does this mean to you?

OK, to me, resilience can be physical. It can also be mentally, emotionally, and psychologically. We saw on day two of the first deployment it was cold, and some of the most physically strong SATs suffered from the cold and had to go home because it was making them ill. So, it's about being physically resilient as well as psychologically resilient. (The SAT members were from a hot country deploying to a cold one).

Being an SAT is also about being able to work with traumatised families and being able to switch off at the end of a shift. If you can't switch off, then it just builds up, and you end up having to be sent home. Being able to talk to your fellow SATs about your day or your team leader is important. Listening to music, reading, exercising or whatever you like to do is so important to make sure you can emotionally cope with each day and what it holds.

Sometimes, calling home and just '*touching base*' is good as well. Not offloading your day because you can't do that, but hearing about what's going on at home is a good way to switch off and decompress.

You have to be able to endure long days and little rest. You have to be able to be on top form each day for your family and be there for them and not be complaining about how tired or hungry or cold you are. It's just two weeks for you, but for them, it's a lifetime, so resilience is also about it not being about you but about them and being able to put your issues aside for a while. Not everyone can do that.

You deployed to two high-profile accidents one after another. How did you cope with that?

The training and exercises don't really prepare you for that. The deployments were so different as well. You deploy to one, and you think you know how it's going to be, but then you deploy again, and it's so different that you have to relearn everything. Every deployment is unique.

When I got the call for the second deployment, it was like, '*OK. I've got this*', but really, when you go, it's different languages, different cultures, different demographics and location, so nothing is the same as the last time. It's a bit of a shock. You run on adrenalin a lot, especially when you get the initial call.

How did the two HACs differ?

They were really different because for the first deployment, the families were already there waiting for us, but for the second one, we had time to set things up, and fewer families came. They stayed at home. Two very different cultures (one Asian and one European). The second one was harder than the first one, strangely enough, because I didn't have time to think. When we arrived, families were there, and we just switched to SAT mode, but for the second one, we were waiting for the families to arrive, so it was nerve-wracking.

For the first HAC, we got on a plane specially set aside for us and the Go team. When we landed, we went straight to work with no sleep, and we worked purely on adrenalin.

No one slept on the flight because everyone was too hyped, so by the time we landed, it was nearly 24 hours into the accident.

The culture, language and religion were so different as well. It was hard to know how to support the families. They were so angry and distressed. How we managed was to run the family briefings regularly, as the training taught us. Twice a day. Slowly, we got into a routine, and the families started to trust us. In the second HAC, we didn't run them as regularly as there were fewer families, so we ran them once a day.

What was the process for the HAC closing down?

Well, actually, the first HAC stayed open for about five months, with SATs rotating in and out. We also set one up in the home country of the largest number of families once we closed down with regular meetings held.

The second one was closed within 17 days as families stayed at home and were much more supported by their government, and we really weren't needed as much.

It felt really weird going home the first time, having been away so long (I stayed as the SAT Manager for the whole five months). The airline was good and got us all together to talk about our experiences and to support us. I had a couple of days off and then went back to work, my choice. I needed to do '*normal things*' and get back into a work/home routine.

It was good to talk to my fellow SAT members. You share an experience that no one else can really understand. Not your family, your work colleagues or friends. Only those who were there can. You have to support each other as you transition back to your lives. It's a surreal experience working at an HAC, but it's one that most SATs would jump at doing again. To help people like that is such an honour.

Returning Home

Part of the training initially should help the SAT members understand that coming home from a deployment is a strange feeling and can make some SAT members feel sad. Obviously, having spent time with families at their worst times and getting close to people means leaving them can be challenging. Rotating SAT members in and out regularly helps to minimise this as families have to get used to a different SAT member, and a returning SAT member would always be given a different family to look after.

Preparing everyone for leaving is vital. At the HAC, once a rotation is going to happen and a date is given for a SAT member to leave, the family is told. They are then reminded regularly (perhaps daily) that '*Sarah*' (for example) '*will be taking over from Ben in five days' time*'. This allows the family to get used to the idea of a new SAT member looking after them.

When '*Sarah*' arrives, she would be introduced to the family, and then for an overlapping day, there would be two SAT members supporting the family. By the end of the day, '*Ben*' would have let '*Sarah*' take over answering questions and perhaps left to pack and complete any admin needed before leaving but still be at the HAC if needed. This includes handing over the SAT manual used to enter meeting details, etc., and business cards and receipts. If the handover is handled smoothly and with compassion, it can be a positive experience for the families and the SAT members.

Clearly, it is always hard to say goodbye, but if the boundaries have been kept and the family understands that this is goodbye with no further contact, then it can be a meaningful goodbye.

 **Observation**

Having undertaken over 40 deployments, it is always hard to say goodbye. I often think of the families I have supported at HACs and wonder how they are doing, but I have never been tempted to contact them. My understanding is that my presence in their life could be a negative trigger long-term, which makes me understand that it is not possible.

If a family contacted me via Facebook/Meta® or another social media platform, I would not reply and decline a friend request. It seems and indeed feels harsh, but it is psychologically best for them and for me.

Transitioning to Home and Work

SAT members often take a while to get used to being at home or going back to work. As the interviewee in Case Study 4 said, *'It felt really weird going home the first time'*, and airline post-accident support is vital for an easier transition back into the workplace. Having time set aside to talk about their experiences with fellow SAT members, to allow them to give feedback on the process, how they were managed, how they experienced the deployment, etc., allows for every-one involved to '*process*' the role at the HAC, hospital or family home and any issues that may have arisen (Norwood, Ursano & Fullerton, 2000). Airlines can learn a lot from these events to make changes to recruitment, training and ongoing support. Having an airline leadership that champions the support of returning SAT members can contribute to the overall success of an accident operation and the longer-term quality of the SAT moving forward.

Deployment is not a negative experience in most cases. Often, the SAT member can experience a positive development of skills, experience, resilience and personal growth **IF** it is managed well by the airline (Qin & En, 2018).

Post-Traumatic Growth

Briefly, this is when an experience that could potentially be traumatic causes a cognitive shift in someone's brain to allow them to see the benefits and positives of what has happened. Building resilience and coping strategies for future events and personal wellbeing of the individual (Tedeschi & Calhoun, 1998). This book will not go into detail on this topic, but it is something that happens to those who respond to accidents in some cases and should be borne in mind for airline SAT members.

Conclusions

Being a SAT member is a core part of a deployment for the airline. Airlines have to have them, and although the numbers might be supplemented by TPPs, they are still the airline representative at the HAC, hospital or family's homes.

How the SAT members are recruited, trained and prepared for their role is key to a successful deployment. Understanding what is expected of them, the boundaries set and some of the potential issues they may have to deal with is part of an airline's responsibility for their teams.

Each deployment is different, and each is unique, but the key themes that come out of each one remain the same. These are things that can be taught beforehand. SAT members have to interact with many agencies and have the skills to communicate through different languages, understanding cultures and sharing their experiences.

Key Points from this Chapter

- SAT members are made up of volunteers from the airline and may have very different roles in normal operation. They should have a range of skills and qualities and be willing to undertake what can be a demanding role
- Training is key with honesty about what they may experience. Giving as much knowledge as possible to help them understand their role. Training should be regular to keep up the skills and consider new SAT members initial training experience
- Bringing a TPP to share their experiences and undertake the training can help with this as it bridges the theory and the reality of the role. Also, consider bringing in family associations to share their experiences as a service user
- TPP and airline SAT members should exercise together if they are likely to deploy together. This helps with trust and building skills and understanding between the two teams
- Understanding that not everyone is able or willing to volunteer for this role is also key. Not everyone would want to undertake this role or be able to do it. That is fine, and there are plenty of other key tasks a staff member can do in an accident operation that does not require them to deploy
- Airlines need to have a well-developed post-accident support system in place for returning SAT members. To help them understand what they have experienced, collect and analyse feedback to make the necessary changes to training or processes and to support their transition back into the workplace

Exercise

A SAT member comes to you (her manager) and is concerned that she has received a 'friend request' through Facebook/Meta® from a family she met during a deployment several times but has declined it only to find it back there the next week. They are worried about replying to them (they have not replied) and do not want to appear rude, but understand they should not carry on the supportive relationship outside the HAC. She asks you what she should do.
   What option would you pick?

1. Tell them to 'block' them and move on.
2. Talk to them about their worries but tell them it is OK to be a friend on Facebook/Meta® as it's not like seeing them in real life, and no one would ever find out, so what would be the harm?
3. Contact the family as the SAT Manager and gently remind them that SAT members are not permitted to have contact with the families they support at the HAC and to please not contact the SAT member again with a request. Direct any support they may want to the longer-term contact email address.

Answer – 3. Sometimes, it is best to be clear about expectations as a *'duty of care'* for both parties.

Notes

1 Care team is a term used interchangeably with SAT. Some airlines are now using Care team instead, but ICAO still use the term 'SAT'.
2 An example might be STAR alliance that has *'partners'* all over the world and often *'codeshares'* on flights. They may be able to take on short term support until the Go Team and/or SAT members arrive.
3 These A5 size manuals have space for notes, pockets to collect business cards at meetings from officials and envelopes for receipts. The SAT is expected to complete these notes for every single meeting and decisions made, and then they are given back at the end of a rotation to be given to the inquiry as evidence of how the airline supported survivors and families. Often called *'the little black book'* due to their colour.
4 Similar to when visitors use headsets to translate a guide around an attraction. The individual can hear the presentations, questions and answers in their chosen language simultaneously with the presentation itself.

References and Additional Reading

Family Assistance Act. (1996/2000). (Online). Available at: www.ntsb.gov/tda/er/Pages/tda-fa-aviation. aspx.
Norwood, A. E., Ursano, R. J., & Fullerton, C. S. (2000). Disaster Psychology: Principles and Practice. *Psychiatric Quarterly*, 71 (3) pp. 207–226. https://doi.org/10.1023/A:1004678010161.
Qin, L. Q., & En, D. T. S. (2018). Counsellors in Crisis Management: A Malaysian Case Study. *International Journal of Choice Theory and Reality Therapy*, 38 (1) pp. 37–45.
Quevillon, R. P., Gray, B. L., Erickson, E. D., & Jacobs, G. A. (2016). Helping the Helpers: Assisting Staff and Volunteer Workers Before, During, and After Disaster Relief Operations. *Journal of Clinical Psychology*, 72 (12) pp. 1348–1363. https://doi.org/10.1002/jclp.22336.
Rowntree, G., & Akerlund, M. (2012). Turning Training into Reality: Considerations When Training Teams for Deployment to Disasters. In R. Hughes, A. Kinder, & C. L. Cooper (Eds.). *International Handbook of Workplace Trauma Support* (pp. 401–415). London: Wiley Blackwell.
Tedeschi, R. G., & Calhoun, L. G. (1998). Posttraumatic Growth: Conceptual Issues. In R. G. Tedeschi, C. L. Park, & L. G. Calhoun (Eds.). *Posttraumatic Growth: Positive Change in the Aftermath of Crisis* (pp. 1–22). Mahwah, NJ: Lawrence Erlbaum Associates.

6   Airport Response

Chapter Objectives

In this chapter, you will be able to:

- Explain the initial duties of the airport if an accident takes place in the vicinity
- Demonstrate you understand the different centres in the airport and what they offer
- Describe the flow of passengers after an accident
- Understand where the survivors, crew and families are transferred to once the airport operation starts to close down

Opening Quiz

1. How are airports involved in aviation accident operation?
2. How do rescue services ensure information is gathered about those involved whilst triaging injured passengers?
3. How long does the airport need to support families and survivors until they can transfer to the HAC?
4. What kind of support must the airport be prepared to offer those impacted by the accident?

Glossary for this Chapter

CMC   Crisis Management Centre
EMC   Emergency Management Centre (Airport)
ICAO International Civil Aviation Organization
HAC   Humanitarian Assistance Centre
TEC   Telephone Enquiry Centre
TPP   Third Party Provider

Chapter Introduction

Although accidents may take place in any location, this chapter concentrates on when an accident takes place at the airport, —either at departure, arrival, stop-over or if used for an emergency landing.

DOI: 10.4324/9781003405337-9

As part of ICAO Doc 9998 (2013), airports are required to have comprehensive emergency plans that include how they will support passengers involved in an accident, families of those involved and the media within the terminal. Airports and airlines should work together to ensure the staff are trained and plans are exercised regularly so that everyone is aware of each other's roles and how everything works in harmony. These exercises should be multi-agency, giving all parties that would have to work together in such an event the opportunity to test their own plans and understand some of the complexities of a multi-agency approach for personnel who, in the beginning, are to treat passengers who may be injured, as well as gather as much information about those involved to help identify passengers from the manifest (Janev, Mijović, Tomašević, Kraus & Vraneš, 2012). The plans should be audited regularly, as discussed in Chapter 2, and the airports must have proper arrangements to ensure they can support families and survivors during the first 24 hours of an accident or before they transfer to the HAC, whichever is sooner. During an accident, they must also have plans that deal with the other passengers at the airport, not involved in any way efficiently and whilst responding to the accident operation taking place (Tidah, 2019).

The core responsibility of an airport during an accident is to ensure all passengers on the manifest are accounted for either via hospital transfer, mortuary or uninjured survivors. This is extremely complicated to do as identification of the deceased will not have taken place at this time. Ensuring the identification of survivors is a step towards fulfilling these requirements. By working closely with other agencies and authorities, it is possible to give a clear picture of the situation.

Airports are busy commercial operations, and dealing with an accident within the airport vicinity can be challenging as it requires resources, rooms and access to airside facilities. Airports are also '*open access*' landside, making them easily accessible for families who are concerned and the media who may be arriving. For large airports, this can be accommodated with specific areas set aside, but for smaller airports, this can mean considerable impact on the location and surrounding areas and may need temporary structures such as marquees to be erected to support such an operation.

The Family Assistance Act (1996/2000) requires an airport to have set aside several '*rooms*' to be available to accommodate the variety of parties that need to support and manage the initial phase of the operation. This is at the same time as the Crisis Management Centre (CMC) is being set up and activated, so close coordination with the CMC is vital at this early stage as well as the Telephone Enquiry Centre (TEC) to take calls. By close coordination between these centres, a good picture of the developing situation can start to emerge.

However, depending on the size of the accident itself and how many people are impacted, the use of other areas such as offices, warehousing and other such facilities may need to be considered (Polatar, 2020).

The airport also needs an emergency management room, usually called an 'Airport Emergency Management Centre' or more commonly referred to as an 'EMC'.[1] This could be located anywhere in the airport but is usually '*landside*' due to the restricted access required for passing through to '*airside*'. This is the airport equivalent of the airline CMC and '*oversees*' the airport response to the accident.

The airport must also have other '*key areas*' that need to be '*scaled up*' in response around the airport.

This includes:

- Survivors Centre
- Family and Friends Centre

- A crew reception centre
- Reunification centre
- Media centre

Identification of those Involved

At the site of an accident, it is vital that triage is given quickly. However, it is also important to understand who is injured so everyone on board can be accounted for and families offered the most accurate and up-to-date information about their loved one.

For those who are injured, they will be triaged *'in situ'* and either released to go to the survivors centre at the airport or taken to hospital. Everyone involved in the rescue operation needs to know who these survivors are and where they might be taken if hospital treatment is required.

ICAO Document 9998 (section 3) requires the local authorities and rescue services to be responsible for gathering as much information as possible alongside treating those who have survived. This may be as basic as seat number (if known) or location in the aircraft itself such as economy or next to a window etc.

The information gathered will be passed to the EMC and the airline CMC so families gathered at the airport can be informed. TEC outbound teams will also inform families who have called into the TEC to ask about their loved ones.

This coordinated approach helps to establish numbers, identification of survivors and the whereabouts of the hospitals where they may be being treated. As multiple agencies and rescue services will be involved, the application of the plan as exercised between all the parties becomes vitally important. The information pouring into the various systems and being communicated between the parties is reliant on everyone understanding their role and how they fit into the plan for the rescue of those involved and also how decisions are made from the EMC and airline CMC.

However, this can be a chaotic and high-pressure situation, and the priority of the rescue services would always be the treatment of the survivors. Asking for information on people's names and the location of the hospital they are taking them to can sometimes understandably be missed. Therefore, the information can be delayed as the hospitals may have to be the agency that enters the information required. This initial stage of an accident is critical and can be the *'most complicated due to the lack of information'* (Guo, Zhang, Zhang & Meng, 2018: 2).

Another complex issue can be if people have been impacted on the ground but are not passengers or crew. Finally, ensuring all the agencies and their independent systems *'talk'* to each other and gather accurate information can be challenging.

Key Areas During a Response Near the Airport

Survivors Centre

For those who are not injured or who have been treated at the scene and released, they will need somewhere to be taken for support and to help the authorities with the initial investigation. The Survivor Centre will be expected to supply basic fresh clothing, food and water. Survivors will not have their baggage with them, so many also need medication, identification if they have nothing on them and perhaps even house and car keys.

Survivors will talk to the authorities and will have their identifications verified, as well as receive medical help to ensure they are OK to leave. Counsellors will also be on hand to offer help where they can as well as immigration services to help with identification and issue temporary visas if the survivor needs to go to the hospital or HAC or stay in a local hotel before carrying on their journey or going home. The need for interpreters that can understand cultural and religious requirements is also key in the centre (Alexander & Pescaroli, 2018).

The centre will be *'airside'*, which means it is beyond the normal security and immigration stages and near to the airport apron area and, therefore, protected from face-to-face media intrusion, but at this point, they will not have immediate access to their loved ones who will be waiting for them in the reunification centre which will be landside.

The Survivors Centre will often be resourced by trained airport volunteers or Third Party Providers (TPP) experienced staff if they have local coverage and can get instant and temporary access to *'airside'*. The Family Assistance Act (1996/2000) and ICAO Doc 9998 mandates that there must be a trained team ready to undertake this work.

Family and Friends Centre

This will be positioned *'landside'*, which is before the security and immigration stages and near the airport entrances and is where the friends and families of those on board will be taken once an accident has been confirmed. The accident does not necessarily need to be at the airport for the centre to be opened, but the airport would need to be involved in the flight in some way, either as the departure or arrival destination.

The Family and Friends Centre must be a secure space to ensure media and other passengers do not have access to the area. This is where those who have come to the airport worried about their loved ones can gain further information from the airport staff, authorities and other agencies.

If their loved ones have survived and are either in a hospital or in the survivor centre, this is where they will be told by trained staff or the authorities.

Crew Reception Centre

This would be for the uninjured crew to be able to receive treatment and support in the same way as the passengers but also for the authorities to more *'formally'* interview them about what happened. This could be the local police, intelligence services or military. They are kept separate from the passengers because of being interviewed but must also be offered the same services that passengers are offered. They would also be offered support from a trained team.

Crew and especially flight crew can offer more detailed, specialist and specific information about the aircraft, accident and subsequent evacuation or rescue that passengers would not be able to offer.

Reunification Centre

Unless the airport is large enough to have its own Reunification Centre, the most obvious place to have this is in the arrivals area.

This would most likely be landside (but not always), where the uninjured survivors can meet with their relatives in privacy and away from the media. Of course, this reunification will not apply to all families, and for those whose loved ones are not on the list of injured or uninjured survivors, they will be transferred to where their loved ones have been taken or transferred to the HAC once this has been agreed. This can take a while to establish, so airports must take care of these families until such a time the Humanitarian Assistance Centre (HAC) can support them adequately. This can be up to 24 hours. Fig 6.1 illustrates the flow of passengers post triage to one of the options set up by the authorities. To the Survivor Centre, triaged on site then released to the Survivor Centre, triaged and transferred to hospital or to the mortuary.

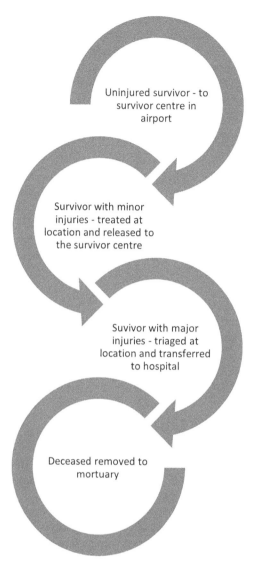

Figure 6.1 Flow of survivors from crash site

Families who are being united with their loved ones can then leave the airport but will be offered follow-up support from the airline. Either driven home (people involved are discouraged from driving) or travel arrangements made to fly on to their destination (if they wish to). Follow-up counselling will be offered, and any bills resulting from the accident will be met by the airline. Any baggage recovered will also be sent to them.

Media Centre

For all accidents that include an airport, there will be an area or a room set up to support the requirements of the media. This can be to issue statements, answer questions and generally enable media to get information out to the public.

This will always be landside, away from the Reunification Centre, and may be a self-contained media centre with IT and technology already included or, if a smaller or more remote airport, then an area to receive information from the airport authorities.

Media are not allowed into any of the other centres at the airport, but if families and survivors wish to talk to the media, they can do so by going to the media centre or leaving the airport terminal.

Closing Airport Operations and Transferring to the Humanitarian Assistance Centre

Within the first 12–24 hours, the operation at the airport to rescue and recover those involved will start to transfer to the HAC where the airline takes full responsibility to support the uninjured survivors, those with minor injuries and families of the deceased. They will also transfer the surviving crew to their HAC facility as well.

The operation to recover any wreckage at the airport may well take a lot longer, but the first stage of the rescue has taken place and now the HAC can support families arriving as well for those who have been notified their loved ones were on the passenger manifest.

Depending on any damage to runways or if the airport has supported the accident as part of the aircraft routing, it can be back to '*normal*' operations within 24 hours and then take a more supportive role of bringing in families to the HAC. It still needs to communicate with the HAC, but at this time, the EMC could be closed down and the airport's involvement would rapidly decrease.

Some of the trained staff might temporarily transfer to help open the HAC if they can be spared from the operation, but if the airline and the TPP have enough trained resources then this would not be necessary.

Conclusions

The airport is often the first phase of a disaster operation, even if the accident takes place in a different location. This is because families and friends often say goodbye if it's at the departing airport or waiting for the aircraft to arrive.

The airport is required by regulation to support the families for between 12–24 hours as part of their plans. It is a much shorter involvement in the operation, but it is crucial for understanding the initial situation, identifying the survivors and where those who have been injured are taken for medical attention and supporting families and survivors before the HAC opens.

This part of the operation includes multiple agencies and parties who must work closely together to ensure a coordinated response. Gathering information about those being treated or moved is essential to reconcile the passenger manifest and give family and friends accurate information about their loved ones. Working closely with the airline CMC, the TEC and the HAC is key to the airport being the initial focus of any accident.

Key Points from this Chapter

- Airports are a key partner in the whole accident response and have a vital part to play in the initial phase of the operation
- Having trained staff who can support the survivors and families and friends of those impacted by an accident is a requirement, as per legislation, as is having rooms set aside for the key areas required

- Some airports would struggle to ensure the required rooms would be available if they are small, or remote airports and may need to use other buildings or temporary structures
- The airport must support those involved for up to 24 hours or until the HAC is open and ready to receive people

Quiz

Take a few minutes to complete this quiz to check your understanding of this chapter.

1. Which legislation does the airport's responsibilities in an accident come from?
2. Why is it important to move families waiting for news of their loved ones away to a quieter and more secure area?
3. If the airport is too small to house the required areas to support survivors and families, what else could be considered?
4. What are the three key challenges that rescue agencies have when treating survivors?
5. What is the flow of the passengers and crew to locations in the airport?
6. How long is it usually before the airport will transfer survivors, crew and families to the HAC?
7. Where will the media centre be set up, and what is its purpose?
8. Why are the surviving crew separated from other survivors? Who might want to interview them? And what for?

Note

1 EMC – An Emergency Management Centre at the airport works in the same way as the CMC works for an airline. It coordinates the initial rescue response if the accident is in the vicinity of an airport. All emergency centres open will communication with each other.

References and Additional Reading

Alexander, D. E., & Pescaroli, G. (2018). The Role of Translators and Interpreters in Cascading Crises and Disasters Towards a Framework for Confronting the Challenges. *Disaster Prevention and Management*, 29 (2) pp. 144–156. https://doi.org/10.1108/DPM-12–2018–0382.

Family Assistance Act. (1996/2000). (Online). Available at: www.ntsb.gov/tda/er/Pages/tda-fa-aviation.aspx.

Guo, Y., Zhang, S., Zhang, Z., & Meng, Q. (2018). Estimating Added Values of the Integrated Emergency Response System for Airport Accident: Improved Responsiveness and Increased Service Capacity. *Mathematical Problems in Engineering*, 2018. https://doi.org/10.1155/2018/3960242.

ICAO. (2013). *Assistance to Aircraft Accident Victims and Families, Doc 9998/499*. Montreal: International Civil Aviation Organization.

Janev, V., Mijović, V., Tomašević, N., Kraus, L., & Vraneš, S. (2012). Dynamic Workflows for Airport Emergency Management Training. *23rd International Workshop on Database and Expert Systems Applications*. https://doi.org/10.1109/DEXA.2012.43.

Polatar, A. (2020). Airports' Role as logistics Centres in Humanitarian Supply Chains: A Surge Capacity Management Perspective. *Journal of Air Transport Management*, 83 (1). https://doi.org/10.1016/j.jairtraman.2020.101765.

Tidah, R. (2019). Airport Emergency Management: The Art of Strict Rules and Flexible Minds. *Journal of Business Continuity & Emergency Planning*, 13 (3) pp. 230–239.

7 Humanitarian Assistance Centre (HAC)

Chapter Objectives

By the end of this chapter, you will be able to:

- Explain what a HAC is and why it is important in a response operation
- Describe who might come to the HAC for the services provided
- Demonstrate an understanding of how a HAC might be set up
- Explain what the key services are that are provided at the HAC
- Understand and describe the boundaries that are in place for working at the HAC

Opening Quiz

1. What is a HAC?
2. What is the core purpose of an HAC?
3. Who would go to the HAC?
4. What kind of support services are offered at the HAC?
5. Who works at the HAC to support families and survivors who are staying there?

Glossary for this Chapter

DVI	Disaster Victim Identification
FAC	Family Assistance Centre
HAC	Humanitarian Assistance Centre
ICAO	International Civil Aviation Organization
INTERPOL	International Criminal Police Organization
NTSB	National Transportation Safety Board
SAT	Special Assistance Team
TEC	Telephone Enquiry Centre

Chapter Introduction

The Humanitarian Assistance Centre or HAC is often used as a term interchangeably with Family Assistance Centre (FAC). Various agencies and authorities prefer using one over the other. For the purposes of this book, they mean the same thing, but HAC is the preferred term used here.

DOI: 10.4324/9781003405337-10

The HAC is a secure and safe space for survivors and families of those who are injured or who are deceased, who can come to the named centre at the expense of the airline to gain direct information and updates about the investigation, the process of recovery of their loved one, personal effects and salvage of the wreckage. They come for news and support (Easthope, 2022).

Those who attend are named and linked to a passenger on the manifest in the case of the deceased. Identity has been verified either via the Telephone Enquiry Centre (TEC) or via the authorities so the HAC teams know who to expect and when to expect them.

The HAC can be a hotel, which is usual, but it does depend on the location though a hotel is always preferred given the infrastructure needed to run a potentially large support operation. However, in some smaller locations such as the Caribbean or in locations where a hotel might not be suitable due to lack of infrastructure, the following can also be utilised (Brown, Efthymiou & McMullan, 2022):

- University or college student halls
- Civic amenities such as hostels and offices
- Holiday resorts
- Use of a business or conference centre for daytime services with remote accommodation elsewhere

For this book, an assumption will be made that a large enough hotel will be used for a HAC that can accommodate everyone on site and has a large enough conference centre or room to use for the family briefings.

It is normal for survivors to have their own HAC that may be separate from the families of those who are deceased. This is because the needs of the two groups may well be distinct. For the purposes of this chapter, it will assume a family HAC, but the services offered would be exactly the same for survivors.

Humanitarian Assistance Centre Overview

The specific services offered can vary for each situation, but the skills and teams required as well as the resources to run these services will also need to vary and may be pre-requisite to opening or managing a HAC as Table 7.1 clearly shows.

The NTSB has a useful schematic that can help with understanding what services and areas need to be set up and offered in an HAC. And this is detailed in Figure 7.1.

Note – the schematic uses the term FAC, but it is the same as HAC.

Depending on the size of the response operation, not all rooms or services might be required, but initially, they should be planned for and part of the setting up process, pre-opening. To explain the HAC operations each service or room will be explored in more detail.

Family Briefing Room

As introduced in Chapter 5, the family briefings take place on a daily or twice daily occurrence. At the beginning of a response, having more than one briefing a day can be helpful to catch arriving families until a routine can be established.

The family briefing MUST take place once a day for everyone at the same time. This is so the families all hear the updates from the agencies first, before anyone else, i.e., the media. It is not permissible as part of the Family Assistance Act (1996/2000) to have several '*sittings*' so the room used should be large enough to accommodate everyone who needs to attend in one go.

Table 7.1 Pre-requisite skills and teams working in a HAC

Pre-Requisite Skills Required	Team	Additional Skills (may need to be outsourced or require further training)
Setting up and managing a HAC	Management team	IT, HR, data analysis and reporting. Health and Safety (if required) risk assessment, policies and procedures
Languages and experience of international cultures	Admin team	Experience dealing with different demographics and potentially an understanding of geopolitics
Logistics	Logistics or linked to Transport	Supply chain knowledge
Finance	Finance	Accountancy or financial data gathering, reporting and analysis
Accommodation	Hotel Services	Hotel management, cultural skills
Childcare	SAT Management	Childcare qualifications
Mental Health	Management team	Qualifications and license to practice
Transport	Transport or linked to Logistics	Supply chain knowledge

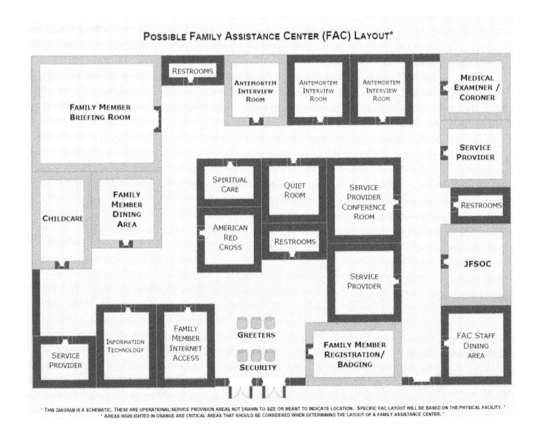

Figure 7.1 NTSB suggested layout for required services or rooms in an HAC

Reproduced courtesy of the NTSB

This is a core consideration when deciding where to house a HAC. However, if the operation is large and there are no hotels that can accommodate such a requirement, it might be more suitable to have the HAC and accommodation in one place with access to, and transport to, another location specifically to hold the family briefings such as a conference centre or similar.

How you set up the family briefing room will depend largely on the numbers expected to attend.

For smaller numbers, a *'café style'* setting might be more appropriate as Figure 7.2 shows each table can have tissues, water, etc., with a top table set aside for the presenters along with the technical facilities required to update everyone on the investigation, etc. Having a separate door for the presenters to leave by can be more appropriate than having them walk through the families or survivors, but this is purely for security considerations.

The entrance for the families and survivors would need to be secure as well to ensure media or uninvited guests cannot gain access. Access would be by an identification badge only, and this will be described in more detail later on in this chapter.

Translators would also sit at the top table. If there is space, having a SAT member with a portable microphone can aid questions from the floor to the presenters.

Note – windows in a family briefing room should be covered up to keep the meeting private for the families and survivors and away from media or uninvited but interested parties.

For Larger numbers, see Figure 7.3.

This setting is called *'cinema style'* and involves rows of chairs with a gap down the middle or in sections to ease access and egress. The challenge for this is the formality of the rows,

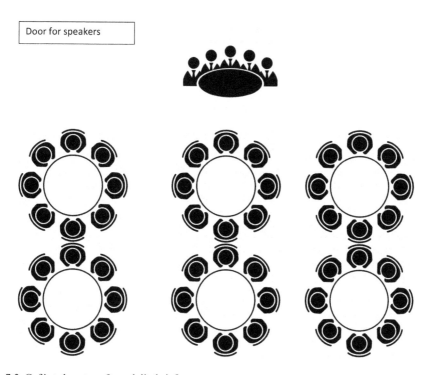

Figure 7.2 Café style set up for a daily briefing

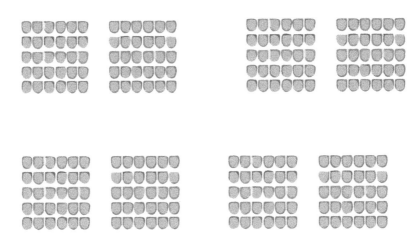

Figure 7.3 Cinema style set up for a family briefing

along with difficulties in asking questions via a portable microphone and how to access the refreshments.

See Chapter 5, Special Assistance Teams, for how a daily briefing is undertaken.

Meet and Greet Reception Area

As the families arrive at the HAC, having been met at the airport or train station by the SAT members allocated to meet them, they will come to the *'Meet and Greet'* desk. This is, in essence, a focused check-in area resourced by experienced staff who know the families are arriving, who they are linked to on the passenger manifest and, therefore, do not need to explain who they are, etc.

The reasons for having a separate area away from the hotel operations are twofold. First, to give the hotel reception staff the ability to carry on with their operation as the hotel may have other guests staying there. This is not the case in the US, as Federal law does allow for a hotel to be *'cleared'* for humanitarian assistance, but the rest of the world may have to share the hotel and its facilities with non-HAC guests.

The reception staff may not know or understand the reason for the new guests arriving and could ask questions that further distress the families arriving in innocence. To minimise this for all parties, having a discreet and private area tucked away means the arriving families can be assured of a safe space on arrival.

The second reason for having a distinct space away from reception is that the hotel staff may well not be trained or experienced in dealing with distressed or traumatised people, and it would be unfair and unreasonable to ask them to deal directly with the families when the HAC has a trained team that can do it.

The *'meet and greet'* area should be away from reception, in a secure and private location that can accommodate two staff and be a sensitive and calm area for the families to check in to the HAC and talk to them about the services that are offered, family briefing times, language or cultural requirements and what they might need from the Special Assistance Team (SAT) members allocated to them.

Often, families do not know what the HAC does or why it is open when they arrive. They are offered the chance to go to the HAC and may arrive unsure of what to expect. Having a calm and comfortable *'meet and greet'* area with people who know why they are there and can help them whilst they are staying decreases what could be a negative first impression of the HAC.

Packs are created to give to arriving families in different languages as families in distress often do not recall information given initially. The pack includes everything explained by the *'meet and greet'* team. Timings, locations, services available, etc., should be included in the pack, and the allocated SAT member will then guide the family around the HAC to orientate them and help them get to their room.

The *'meet and greet'* area would be resourced by two staff 24/7 initially as it can be a good location for families to call or come to if they need anything during the night. It is often the place they remember, as it was the first place they went to when they arrived. As the operation scales down, the operation hours for the area can be decreased accordingly.

Badging

This task can often sit within the *'meet and greet'* area so that as each family arrives, they can be given an identification badge with a lanyard to allow access to the *'secure'* areas such as the family briefing room or childcare, etc. Access would be restricted due to sensitivities around the safety of everyone moving around the HAC, so it is important that everyone involved in the response, from families to SAT members, need to have an identifying lanyard and badge. Often, badges are supplied with photos taken at the time, and all arriving families would be asked to bring their own identification when arranging their travel at the Telephone Enquiry Centre (TEC) or through the airline to support this process.

To make quick identification easier, each lanyard is coloured, so it is easy to know who is a family member, who is working at the HAC and what area they are working in. For example, family members might all have yellow lanyards, making them easy to quickly identify. SAT members might have green, etc.

Access to the daily briefings would include checking badges, but clearly, sensitivity around families would also balance this as not permitting a family member to a daily briefing because they have forgotten their badge could be distressing. SAT members can support this as they would know the families they are supporting. Clearly, if no one knows who the individual is, and they want access to the daily briefing but have no badge, then they would need to be refused access in case they are media or an uninvited guest until identification can be confirmed.

Incident Management Centre at the Humanitarian Assistance Centre

As detailed in Chapter 3, the Incident Management Centre (IMC) is usually set up at the HAC so that it can take over the management of the response operation from the Crisis Management Centre (CMC). Some of the team from the CMC may transfer over to the IMC, or it could be a completely different team. Once the IMC is up and running, the CMC will scale down and act as a support centre for the IMC for equipment, resources or other operational requests. Sometimes, the IMC may need to be *'housed'* in a different location if the HAC cannot support it or the location of the HAC is not close to the location of the crash site.

The IMC is where the main parties, agencies and authorities will locate themselves to ensure a private area for discussions and decision-making. However, this may also take place in the JFSOC, which stands for Joint Force Special Operations Command and is a US requirement under the Family Assistance Act (1996/2000).[1]

Outside the US, although it is best practice, there may not be a JFSOC, and the IMC will fill that requirement to have a private and secure space for the investigation teams and other agencies to talk to each other, communicate information and make decisions.

Again, this area should be open 24/7 and resourced accordingly. Access would be restricted, and security needs to be included for operational reasons. Families and uninvited guests would not be able to gain access.

Operations Centre and Special Assistance Team Operations

Often, there is a second operations '*office*' set up in the HAC. Not to be confused with the IMC, this area is for the day-to-day running of the HAC and is concentrated on SAT member whereabouts, flight teams working on who is arriving, where from, on what airline, etc., as well as booking flights for rotating staff and families or survivors leaving. The personnel working here needs to be trained in flight booking systems and is often undertaken by the airline team or the TPP team with airline booking experience. SAT members would be able to see when their '*family*' arrives and organise transport with logistics and a taxi to the airport to meet them.

Within the SAT operations centre, a logistics and transport team would be accommodated, ready to organise taxis for families going to meetings with the authorities, coaches for site visits, shopping visits for equipment or items required for the office, etc. This could include flowers requested by families for a HAC memorial service, mobile phone SIMs needed locally, medication requested by a SAT member for their family and other requests that would be sourced by the logistics and transport team.

If the daily briefings have to be '*housed*' in a separate building, then logistics and transport teams would also organise and manage any transportation requirements to and from the briefings.

SAT members would also report to the operations centre if they were leaving the building with a family for a meeting or a visit. The time would be logged with a contact number and when the SAT member was due back. If the SAT member and family do not return at the given time, the SAT member would be called. The SAT member would report back to the operations centre at the end of an off-site meeting or visit to report themselves back safely. This way, a '*duty of care*' for SAT members and families can be maintained at all times when outside the HAC.

Other Teams

Finance has a role here in that they would deal with the financial requests from families or SAT members for taxis, food when outside the HAC, items for a child, etc., that would need an invoice but for which the families would not need to pay. The amount and list of items that can be requested through the finance team would be agreed upon early, and definitely before the HAC opened, via the insurance company and airline. Anything that might fall out of the agreed list would be requested on a case-by-case basis to the airline for them to consider and agree. An example might be a trip for a family to go to a theme park for the day with lunch and transport that might exceed the '*request limit*'. Although it might seem a strange request from a HAC, it could be the family needs some space from the HAC and has a small child that needs time with their parents away from the distress. This would be considered a reasonable request but would need to be sanctioned by the airline.

Accommodation and food can be resourced from the operations centre. Any issues around expenses, problems with rooms, special dietary needs and checking in and out can be handled by this team. Not only for the families and survivors staying at the HAC but also for any of the responders, SAT members and airline staff staying there as well. This team works closely with the hotel to ensure everything runs smoothly and nothing is missed or accidently charged to a family, i.e., watching a film if this is an agreed expense whilst staying at the HAC.

Often, the insurance team that underwrites the policy for the airline will send their own experienced 'Go Team' to work within the HAC. This team is essentially there to answer quickly any of the '*one-off*' requests made by families and survivors or SAT members on the family's behalf. They are also there to pay the '*SDR*' payment linked to the Montreal Convention (see Chapter 1 for more details on this).

Legal teams can also be 'invited' to the HAC to help families with legal advice on areas such as wills, the legal questions around child custody and maintenance, officially informing authorities, i.e., banks and governments of a death (once the positive identification has taken place) and how to determine '*next of kin*' if there are issues of doubt but it is not permitted for families to bring a lawyer with them to stay at the HAC. Families that wish to bring a lawyer can do so, but they should be housed elsewhere and are not permitted to attend the family briefings. Meetings would be taken away from the HAC.

 Observation

Having run several high-profile HACs, the Operations Centre is the heart of the response. It is where everyone working at the HAC checks in every shift and checks out at the end of it. It is where SAT members are allocated their roles and are briefed on specific updates so they are aware of what is going on that day. Although it is a hub of activity, it needs to be welcoming and a place where SAT members can come to ask questions, air their concerns and offer feedback. Where this is located is really important as it needs to be readily accessible for those working there but not be overlooked or easily '*breached*' for security.

Childcare

This is a service that under the Family Assistance Act (1996/2000) is a required service. There should be three distinct areas set aside for the provision of looking after children. The areas are offered to allow parents or carers of children to have somewhere alternative to go when potentially highly distressing meetings such as the family briefing or ante-mortem meetings are taking place that parents or guardians may not want the child to be present for. Or just to get away from a hotel room and allow children to '*play*'.

It is resourced by SAT members at the HAC, but if childcare in its fullest form is required, this would be outsourced to a fully qualified, trained and experienced business locally, if possible. If it is not possible, a provision to support childcare might be accommodated by a request and a search for an experienced SAT member or airline member along with others to support that provision. Unaccompanied childcare would not normally be a service offered at the HAC and is rarely used, except in emergencies.

The three areas can be in different rooms or separated out in one larger area. The three distinct areas are:

- Babies from 0–2yrs
- Children 2–16yrs
- Older children 16yrs+

As their needs can be so different, this space can be challenging to organise and run, but the initial SAT that arrive in the initial phase of the response will bring with them '*kit*' that can help start to set up the area. Soft play toys for the babies, puzzles, etc., for the children and headsets and iPads for the teenagers to watch films (for example).

The room/s must be close to toilets, they must also have security on the entrance doors at all times and access would be by an identification badge. It should also be away from noise and through traffic, so not directly in front of the family briefing room or ante-mortem meeting rooms.

Multi-Faith Room

This is a single room that is a quiet space for prayer or contemplation. The kit bought by the initial SAT would include a selection of the required devotional items required for the main religions in the world, i.e., Bible, Torah, Koran, beads for Catholic prayer, a compass for Islamic prayer rituals, etc.

If space is needed for other religious activities or depending on numbers for a specific religion, a separate room can be set up to accommodate this, i.e., near a bathroom for Muslims to allow for washing.

The multi-faith room would be stripped of furniture except for occasional seating and again needs to be in a quieter location and away from busy spaces. The room is often called a '*spiritual room*' or a '*reflective space*'. These are all the same thing but have interchangeable terminology in different parts of the world.

Family Room

The families staying at the HAC have their own rest lounge set aside where they can come from their rooms or after meetings and mix with other families. Often, families want to make contact with each other, and this room facilitates this. It should be a comfortable area where families can make themselves a hot drink (for example) and have snacks available. Alcohol is not available within the family lounge, but families can drink alcohol in the HAC at the bar, etc. Those working in the HAC are not permitted to drink alcohol for the whole time spent at the HAC. Alcohol for families is not usually an expense picked up by the airline, but this is not a hard and fast rule, so exceptions will apply.

Only families can go into the family lounge. SAT members will only enter it to refresh drinks areas or tidy up. It does not need to be a secure room, but it should be monitored to ensure families are able to access it easily and know it's a private space for them.

There should be comfortable chairs and tables available and large enough to accommodate potentially sizeable groups.

Special Assistance Team Lounge

Conversely, the SAT members also have a lounge allocated to them to relax in between shifts and to mix with other SAT members or airline staff working at the HAC if they are from a TPP. Families are not allowed to come in, and again, no alcohol would be served here.

 Tip

Encourage SAT members to use this room and not go straight to their hotel room at night or after a shift unless they are tired, of course. Talking to other SAT members about their day, talking through problems or concerns and being able to laugh or socialise in a private and discreet area away from the families they are supporting is an important part of being able to 'decompress'.

Medical and Mental Health Team Offices

HACs can be large operational hubs and may need both medical and mental health professionals to support the families and those working at the HAC. They can offer immediate services without having to go outside to access them.

Although mental health professionals will not take on counselling or psychological therapy at the HAC, they can offer guidance on how families might be feeling, contact services local to the families to update them on their position and perhaps put in place more long-term options for their return. The medical staff can support medication and refer the family member to a local clinician if more specialist advice is needed or a specific pharmaceutical drug is required via a more formal visit.

They need to be vetted already and are usually retained by the airline or a Third Party Provider (TPP) for just such an occasion or provided by aid agencies like the Red Cross (in the US).

Aid Agencies

The Red Cross and other agencies can play an important part in a HAC operation. In the US, they form part of the Family Assistance Act (1996/2000) and would be used at the HAC in an SAT-type role or supplementary role supporting the families. In other parts of the world, local aid agencies could be used in the same way, such as the Red Crescent.[2] The use of aid agencies can help if the accident is especially large and resources at the HAC are challenging. They have a range of skills that include languages, cultural expertise and support during a disaster operation.

Ante-Mortem Interview Rooms

The rooms used to talk to families about a variety of topics linked to their loved ones need to be quiet and set away from the rest of the HAC. These can be bedrooms that are converted to take out the furniture to leave tables and chairs, and actually, this can work well as then they can be positioned away from the main rooms, allowing for privacy and quiet, i.e., on a higher floor and, if in one wing, with security positioned to ensure privacy.

The ante-mortem interview rooms are a specific room for families to meet with the investigation authorities, mortuary teams, repatriation teams, personal effects teams, Coroners or MEs, etc. or, in fact, anyone who might want to ask them questions or allow the families to ask specific questions of the teams involved in the operation that they may not encounter every day.

One of the core uses of the rooms is, as the name suggests, to capture details about their loved ones when they were alive (ante) that could support a positive identification. This means the families talk to experienced and trained personnel, usually from the TPP, to work through INTERPOL forms to capture very specific information. A SAT member may be asked to accompany their family, and a translator may also be required. These meetings need to be sensitively handled as they can be distressing for the families. However, often, families feel a sense of '*doing something positive*' during these meetings as their information about their loved one can help positively identify them.

The ante-mortem form is yellow and comes from INTERPOL,[3] and it is a worldwide form used for collating information for missing persons. There is a list of questions that the person conducting the interview (usually TPP) go through and gently gather as much information as the families can give. Table 7.2 has adapted this information including what questions to ask, the options available as potential answers, and extra information to show the complexity of the process.

Table 7.2 Adapted from INTERPOL yellow ante-mortem missing persons form

Question	Options	Notes
What is the relationship of the explainer to the missing person?	Different relationships listed	For blood relatives to give a DNA sample if requested
Has their loved one ever been fingerprinted?	Not just for a police record but also for ex-military, etc.	If yes, then systems can be checked
Have they brought anything with them that might have DNA or fingerprints on it?	Taken as evidence	Families are asked to bring these items with them to the HAC when talking to the TEC
Physical description?	Height, weight, build, etc.	To match with post-mortem information gathered
Colour of hair, type of style, bald?	Coloured, natural or no hair at all	To match with post-mortem information gathered
Any scars or tattoos?	Whereabouts and in what form	To match with post-mortem forms to locate them exactly
Any body parts missing?	I.e., appendix, amputee	To match with post-mortem forms to locate them exactly
Any distinguishing features?	I.e., ears or nose pierced or different coloured eyes	To match a physical examination or X-ray/MRI scan in the forensic areas
What clothing were they wearing, if known?	Departing passenger families may know this	Physical examination in the forensic areas
Have they got any dental records?	Families might not have these but might know the missing person's dentist's details	To contact for a request for dental records, usually via a court or judge
Do they wear glasses or contact lenses?	Family may know a particular brand or make	If found on them
Were they wearing a ring or specific jewellery?	Such as a wedding ring, a watch or pendant	If found on them
Did they have anything with them that could identify them?	A specific bag or wallet with cards in it	If found on them
Ancestry links?	Physical and DNA details	To check for specific markers
Any organs missing or a pacemaker?	Anything that could be distinctive, i.e., one kidney	To match physical examination or MRI scan
If female, had they given birth?	Physical changes	To match physical examination or MRI scan
Any implants?	I.e., breast or other	To match physical examination PLUS cross, refer with implant ID to manufacturer and surgery where implanted

Notifications and Decisions

These rooms can also be used by the various teams working outside the HAC to ask families about their wishes for their loved ones' remains once a positive identification has been made. More detail on a positive identification can be found in Chapter 10. Specific *'notification'* rooms might be used in preference to interview rooms given the severity of the conversations that would take place, but only if space allowed for it.

Families will be given news of a positive identification by the authorities in the interview rooms. They will also be asked about repatriation, personal effects and carriage of their loved one in these discussions as well. The teams and authorities will always offer information and answer the family's questions, but ultimately, the families will decide for themselves what their wishes are, and the teams involved in supporting the families will never offer subjective guidance or lead the families to a decision.

Crew Humanitarian Assistance Centre

The crew families may be allocated a different HAC, but the level of service would be equivalent to the family HAC. The reason crew families are sometimes kept separately (not always) is in case there is any suggestion of malpractice by the crew, and this could cause friction between the two parties. It is extremely rare, but planning for a separate HAC for families and crew is a sensible part of the planning process.

Managing the Humanitarian Assistance Centre on a Day-to-Day Basis

As discussed in detail in Chapter 5, the HAC can be a busy operational building with potentially hundreds of people staying. Not just families and people working in the HAC, but non-HAC guests as well already staying at the hotel.

Managers may have to manage teams they do not know or do not know well, in an unfamiliar environment, in a high-pressure situation and using policies and procedures with which they are not totally familiar (Rowntree & Akerlund, 2012).

Managing the HAC takes an experienced team of senior leaders from the airline to be able to understand what needs are to be met and overcome issues as they arise. The team will be in contact (through the IMC) with the CMC back at the airline to update them regularly (usually twice a day) on what is going on, any individual requests that might need to be approved, i.e., expense outside the limits set by the airline and insurance company. They also meet with other agencies and authorities to update them on the day's actions and themes. By having a multi-party approach to this kind of communication, any decisions on issues can be made. It also allows for cross-communication and means everyone is up to date on the latest information.

Making requests for more SAT members or agreeing that some could come home early due to families leaving after a positive identification means the operation can be appropriately run. The HAC management team can work closely with the insurance team at the HAC. The CMC and other agencies plan for the HAC to close and how that needs to be managed, resourced and organised (see Chapter 11).

Often, the HAC management team has to communicate with embassies or government departments locally to request certain documentation or stamps, and will utilise translators to do this.

There may be a need to have more than one HAC if the accident took place in the sea. An example might be a flight from New York to London that crashes mid-Atlantic. In this scenario, it would be sensible to open two HACs. One in New York and one in London. Each would need to offer the same level of services and be resourced equally to begin with. This can be a challenge for airlines and TPPs, given the resource requirement. Depending on how many passengers and family members came to the two HACs, a decision could then be made to scale one down, i.e., most passengers were from the US, and so the New York HAC is twice as busy as the London one. The London HAC could be scaled down, and the resources sent to New York to support the larger HAC.

Accident Site Visits

Accident site visits can be an important part of the grieving process for some families as they wish to see where their loved one died. However, not all families wish to do this, and the choice is respected at the HAC. Transport will be arranged for those families who wish to go, and logistics will ensure flowers can be available for families to leave at the site. Often, families bring mementoes with them to leave at the accident site and letters.

It is not permitted to walk on the actual crash site itself, and usually, the access is limited to a viewing area. The investigation teams will be informed of a site visit so they can limit their activities on the site until the families leave. Families may also want to conduct religious or cultural practices, and wherever possible, these would be accommodated. Media access would be restricted, and they would not be allowed on the crash site itself.

The survivors may also wish to visit the crash site as part of their own psychological process, and often, these take place separately as the groups have very different needs. However, sometimes it is not feasible to conduct a crash site visit if the terrain is dangerous, remote, out to sea or within a geopolitical conflict area. Some governments may also not permit a visit, and in this case, a ceremony or visit to somewhere as near as possible may be more practical.

When a crash site visit takes place, support in the form of counsellors or mental health professionals, security, medical staff and experienced TPP SAT members will accompany them. No airline SAT member or anyone working at the HAC from the airline should be made to attend a crash site visit.

Memorials at the Humanitarian Assistance Centre

The HAC will often arrange a small memorial whilst families are at the HAC. This usually takes place around day five when most families have arrived, and the authorities are also present.

It is organised by the HAC Management in coordination with the operations staff and the hotel staff. It can be low-key and informal or more formal with a high-profile presence. There are no rules about how this should be conducted, but usually, families can offer flowers and light candles at a specific location set up for a memorial. Officials or the investigation teams, etc., may speak at the event, and it is also a time when search and rescue, hospital and airport teams can be represented.

 Observation

The most moving and beautiful memorials I have attended have been more informal and led by the families. Memorials at the HAC can help families start their grieving journey, allow search and rescue and hospital teams to meet the families and give everyone at the HAC, including those working there, the chance to just stop and take a moment to remember why everyone has volunteered to go there in the first place. They do not need to be high-profile media events to be special and powerful.

Family Website Launch

Whilst at the HAC, the airline or potentially the TPP will launch the family website. This is a specific website that offers information, all the released press statements, questions and answers. It can be created before it is needed and 'hidden' much like a dark site ready to be populated as and when it is needed. It gives the families a login to access it and then has a contact section for queries along with relevant legislation for families to understand, access to reports before they are released to the media and a questions and answers section that explains the process for positive identification, personal effects and repatriation (for example).

Conclusions

The HAC is the centre of the local accident response and is run by the airline or in conjunction with a TPP. Ultimately, the airline retains the responsibility for the HAC management.

The families use the HAC as a safe and secure place to ask the investigating teams any questions they have about the progress of the investigation, the agencies about the general recovery of their loved ones, questions to the airline about payments and compensation, etc.

The variety of services that need to be available for families and the space required means a HAC can become a large operation that needs to be managed and organised to run smoothly. Organising everything from crash site visits to death notifications requires a flexible, calm and skilled workforce willing to take on the tasks required.

Key Points from this Chapter

- HACs are multi-roomed centres for families to gain the information they need and to offer information via interviews for positive identification of their loved one
- Resourcing and rotations in and out of the HAC for staff can be a mammoth operation that the CMC, HR and the airline would need to ensure is constantly reviewed
- SAT members communicate their family's needs to the various teams and ensure they are supported whilst at the HAC by being 'available' to the families when they need them
- Crash site visits are not for everyone, and some families want to go, but others do not. Sometimes, crash site visits are not possible
- Memorials are organised around five days from opening and can be large and formal or smaller and more low-key. Either is fine, depending on the families' wishes and the location

---

Scenario

Consider the following vignette and think about how you would respond. There is no right or wrong answer.

Mrs Clarke has arrived at the HAC with her daughter and son-in-law. Mr Clarke (spouse) died on HGF567 from New York to London. The HAC is in New York. Mrs Clarke is insisting she wants the airline to charter a boat to go to the crash site. This is approximately 300 miles off shore and in February when the seas are rough and the temperatures are freezing.

As part of the Family Assistance Act (1996/2000), if agreed, this offer should then be extended to all families at the HAC, and clearly, this would be dangerous and prohibitive.

A New York judge has decided that no visits to the crash site will be offered due to the safety of everyone involved. This is a legally binding ruling.

How would you explain this to Mrs Clarke, who is very angry and distressed by the judgment and feels it is *'her right'* to go? Think about how and where you would handle this scenario, what you might say to her and how you could talk to her daughter and son-in-law about the judgement and hazards of a journey like this.

Be aware offering this trip is not an option.

Quiz

Take a few minutes to complete this quiz to check your understanding of this chapter.

1. Name four key 'services' offered at a HAC.
2. Do crew families sometimes have a different HAC, and why is this?
3. Is a crash site visit always possible, and if not, why not?
4. Name three teams that work in the HAC.
5. On what day from the HAC opening is the local memorial usually held?
6. How many separate childcare areas should be set up?
7. What colour is the INTERPOL ante-mortem form?

Notes

1 JFSOC – A US requirement for multi-agency decision-making in an emergency response.
2 Red Crescent – Middle East equivalent of the Red Cross.
3 INTERPOL – The International Criminal Police Organisation. Based in Lyon, France, INTERPOL shares data on missing persons across jurisdictions.

References and Additional Reading

Brown, L., Efthymiou, M., & McMullan, C. (2022). Recovering from a Major Aviation Disaster: The Airlines' Family Assistance Centre. *Sustainability*, 14, 4040. https://doi.org/10.3390/su14074040.

Easthope, L. (2022). *When the Dust Settles. Stories of Love, Loss and Hope From an Expert in Disaster*. London: Hodder and Stoughton.

Family Assistance Act. (1996/2000). (Online). Available at: www.ntsb.gov/tda/er/Pages/tda-fa-aviation.aspx.

Rowntree, G., & Akerlund, M. (2012). Turning Training into Reality: Considerations When Training Teams for Deployment to Disasters. In R. Hughes, A. Kinder, & C. L. Cooper (Eds.). *International Handbook of Workplace Trauma Support* (pp. 401–415). London: Wiley Blackwell.

8 Crisis Communications

Chapter Objectives

By the end of this chapter, you will be able to:

- Explain what crisis communications is and why it is so important
- Describe some of the initial tasks and actions needed to comply with aviation regulations
- Understand the different channels for communicating with people in a crisis
- Explain what a 'dark site' is and how it can be used in a crisis

Opening Quiz

1. What is the purpose of crisis communications during an aviation accident?
2. What is the most popular social media platform used for posting a statement?
3. How many minutes from notification of an accident must an airline post a press statement?
4. What is a 'dark site'? What is its purpose?

Glossary for this Chapter

CMC	Crisis Management Centre
HAC	Humanitarian Centre
IATA	International Air Transport Association
IMC	Incident Management Centre
TEC	Telephone enquiry centre
TPP	Third party provider

NOTE – Facebook is now Meta and Twitter is now X; both terms have been used in this chapter for clarity

Chapter Introduction

Crisis communications (crisis comms) is a service that many airlines outsource to expert Third Party Providers (TPP) or specialist companies who are experienced journalists or communications professionals that support clients. Crisis comms includes both internal communications to those who work for the airline at the time of an accident and externally to the wider public and media outlets.

DOI: 10.4324/9781003405337-11

The core job of crisis comms is to anticipate potential themes and challenges or issues for the airline by understanding how the communications channels work, i.e., journalism and social media platforms. They are a link between the airline and the media journalists and help make sure that any communication around the accident is easily accessible, readable and understandable by everyone who reads it or hears it. Crisis comms is also necessary to minimise the risk to the airline brand and reputation (Arokiasamy, Kwaider & Balaraman, 2019). For airlines, crisis comms is necessary to ensure trust in the brand and the safety reputation of the airline can be restored post-accident (Hansson & Vikstrom, 2011). Often, crisis comms experts in this field have a journalistic background, can anticipate the needs and enquiries of the media outlets and have an advanced understanding of how social media platforms work.

The current estimate for worldwide use of social media platforms is over 4 billion people actively using these platforms (Tullett-Prado, Stavropoulos, Gomez & Doley, 2023). The most popular social media platform is Twitter®, now called X®, which is why the guides to crisis comms suggest using Twitter/X® first and expanding social media after that (IATA, 2018).[1] In fact, according to IATA in their 2018 guide, by 2030, in theory, every single person on the planet will have access to social media or at least some kind of network connection.

The aviation industry worked to a '*best practice*' of a '*golden hour*' to have all statements out, offering time to confirm key information in a pre-social media world. The speed of social media has, however, left this far behind and now crisis comms work in '*minutes*' not '*hours*' for initial statements and uses platforms such as Twitter/X® far more to ensure they communicate to as many people as possible in the shortest amount of time.

How Crisis Communications Teams work with Airlines

Airlines retain the service of crisis comms as a distinct contract. This means that when required at the time of the accident, the airline can call on the crisis comms company to guide, advise and analyse the channels of communications that come from the airline and from social media platforms, the TV and newspaper media, internal communications to staff, stakeholders and the families and survivors involved in an incident.

As the long list suggests, the role of the crisis comms team is varied, wide-reaching and extensive. The key to success in any crisis event, be it small or large-scale, for the airline along with the crisis comms team is to understand each other and have a positive working relationship before an activation takes place. Probably more than any other TPP service, crisis comms need to be closely aligned to the airline and especially the senior team to understand the '*internal language*' and culture of the airline. Any communications coming from the airline through the crisis comms team to the outside world needs to sound and read authentically and not sound artificial. This requires time spent together by both parties so that the crisis comms team can train the airline communications team (if they have one), the senior team who will need to be at the forefront of communications through press conferences, '*push*' notifications from the website (those posted to send out information) and social media platforms and through media briefings.

Pre-Activation Actions

By working with the senior management team, especially those who will be involved in the Crisis Management Centre (CMC) for an accident, they can help them to be as ready as possible for media conferences, interviews, social media posts and filmed updates. This may include role-playing different scenarios and questions, such as trying to practice what the media journalists at a press conference might ask. This helps build confidence in what can be an intimidating and high-pressure environment.

Tip

Ensure all of the senior team at an airline has some level of crisis comms training. It can be intense and nerve-wracking having to face the media, and having practiced it beforehand is better than *'learning on the job'*. The public *'expects'* a polished *'performance'* from those who step in front of the camera, and it does help if the team has already made their mistakes and found some confidence before they potentially have to do it.

Templates and Statements

All initial statements can be pre-written (Chandler, 2010). The reason for this is that under the Family Assistance Act (1996/2000), an initial statement needs to be *'tweeted'* onto social media platforms and the website within 15 minutes of a notification of an accident. IATA, in their guide to social media, suggests that

> It has become something of a cliché to observe that "breaking news now breaks on Twitter®". Nonetheless, initial reports of most airline incidents, disruptions or service issues are now most likely to appear online in the form of photos, video or comments from people who experienced it, or those who saw it.
>
> (2018: 4)

This leaves little time to fill in details, and, in fact, the airline might not be in possession of much detail if the accident is not in an obvious place, i.e., ocean or mountains. The initial templated *'tweet'* can read very briefly that the airline acknowledges there is an *'event unfolding'* and that they will offer more information at a stated time. IATA[2] advises within 60 minutes for a fuller explanation. However, consider using platforms such as YouTube®, as they are fast becoming as important.

An example of a templated statement or 'initial *tweet*' could be as simple as:

'ABC Airlines (or '*we*' if preferred) *are aware of a developing situation with one of our aircraft, and we are working hard to establish more detail. As soon as we are able, we will release additional statements'.*

Airlines sometimes include flight numbers, aircraft types and routes but might not know exactly what these are, so keeping it simple is best in the initial phase.

Having these templated statements and posts pre-written means they can be checked and verified ready for use by the airline legal department in advance of using them on the day.

Once the initial statement has been posted, the airline needs to work on updating the information with the toll-free number, any flight details that can be confirmed and other information, such as registration of the aircraft, etc., to be ready within 60 mins of notification.

An example of a templated second *'tweet'* can be found at the end of this chapter.

Of course, depending on the situation, these second tweets can vary, and this one should not be taken as the only version to use. Airlines might not yet be able to confirm the core details, and accuracy is always preferred over speed of communication, but whatever is available and confirmed is helpful for this vital second tweet. Timelines for crisis communications can be seen in Table 8.1.

Other additional information that could be included (within the allowed word count) might be the Captain's name and the hours he/she has flown, hours since aircraft was last in the maintenance hangar and details about the rest of the crew. This is often covered by the media anyway, so if able to confirm, it is often better coming from the airline than a news channel.

Adapted from IATA Guide for crisis communication and reputation management in the digital age (2018).

Use of a Dark Site

This is an area of crisis comms that some airlines employ as part of their plans, and others choose not to. There is no standard right or wrong for this, and it is down to airline choice. Some airlines employ a standard dark site to simplify communications to their customers and those who want information about their loved ones. Other airlines do not and keep their website as normal.

Table 8.1 Timeline for airline communications

Timescale = T + which is notification time	Actions	Issues
15 minutes	First tweet and media statement on website	Very little information available at this stage. Can read as a bland statement
1 hour	Second tweet and further statements on website and social media platforms	May feel panicked about adding more than can be confirmed. ONLY include confirmed information
1 hour	Consider reverting to '*dark site*' if applicable. Add toll-free number to it. Inform Sales and Marketing to stop promotions and review the appropriateness of '*push*' emails to subscription lists	Some airlines do not use '*dark sites*'. Ensure IT, Sales and Marketing are part of the training and exercising so they are aware of the instructions given
3 hours	CEO or nominated spokesperson to appear for the media or filmed update on YouTube® (or similar)	CEO could be on the way to the crash site location or Humanitarian Assistance Centre (HAC), so filming can be a useful '*stop gap*'
6 hours	First press conference from CEO or nominated spokesperson. Apology at this point	Ensure they are ready and do not give out any information that is not confirmed. Some CEOs feel uncomfortable doing this
6–24 hours	Regular press and social media updates. Internal comms sent, more press conference appearances	May have to appear with other agencies, i.e., investigating teams or government representatives
24+	Regular updates, work with Sales and Marketing to ensure all forward promotions are appropriate, monitor social media platforms for themes, etc.	May have to face criticism and social media negativity, especially around '*fake news*'

A dark site is a pre-written site that sits '*behind*' the normal operational site and can be '*brought forward*' during a crisis. It may have muted branding colours or in a grey scale range of tones. One of the reasons for a dark site is to '*dissuade*' masses of curious viewers and to give those who need key information clear directions on how to contact the airline.

The dark site cannot be created during an accident as it takes too long to ensure the colours and messaging are correct. It needs to be created and tested beforehand so that it can easily be implemented when needed. One of the challenges is the need for specific personnel in IT to be available to '*switch on*' the dark site when asked to do so. This means that IT needs to be part of the crisis team to both understand the need for a dark site and their role in activating it.

The dark site essentially '*turns down*' the airline website from full colour and interaction by customers to a more '*muted*' website offering. It switches off some of the interactions between the public and the website. An example might be turning off the ability to buy a ticket for the route or destination of the accident. It can also have the contact numbers (toll-free) and email contact details for the airline for worried family and friends. This is especially helpful to '*signpost*' people to the phone numbers instead of them having to search for them. It may also include a media contact number to filter out the media questions and requests to a specific helpline that can support them.

Having a '*ticker tape*' banner across the bottom of the initial '*tweet*' published and then placed on the site. The reason for doing this is the sheer number of the public that immediately go to an airline website when they hear of a potential crisis event, whatever this might be. This can cause issues for those genuinely impacted members of the public who may not be able to access the information they need because the website can often crash. Having a dark site minimises this and is the main reason that airlines continue to use them at the time of the accident.

Answer machines

Much like a dark site, answering machine messages for areas such as Sales and Marketing can filter out callers to the right phone numbers. Examples can include worried customers who may want to check if their flight is going ahead or if they need reassurance. Although these calls are relevant to those involved, it is important to prioritise those who may be concerned about loved ones first. Having a specific message that clearly tells the caller where to call for their individual needs allows the airline to filter the calls into groupings that can be handled by specific teams.

An example of a suitable answer machine message could be:

'*Thank you for calling ABC Airlines. You are currently unable to leave a message, but if your call is about ABC 123 please re-dial using our toll-free number, which is xxxxxx, and someone will be able to take your call. If you are calling about a future flight, please email us at abc@xxx, and one of our team will reply to you within 24 hours*'.

Again, these messages can be varied in terms of how an airline wants to filter and divert those contacting them, but it is important to note this part of crisis comms can be forgotten in a rush for social media statements and is as important to direct those who call and are concerned about a loved one to the toll-free number.

Crisis Communications Initial Actions

At the time of accident, the crisis comms teams need to be activated at around the same time as the TPP. It could be that they are the same company, but in reality, they are often different organisations due to their distinct expertise. The crisis comms team needs to know the outline of what has occurred so far and what actions have taken place. They can then start to scour social media platforms and begin *'social listening'* (IATA, 2018: 11) for uploaded videos, posts or comments that may help with initial actions. The crisis comms team needs to go initially to the airline's headquarters to support the senior team and communications team to handle (not control) the flow of information in and out of the airline. They may send an additional team to the site of the Incident Management Centre (IMC) to support the HAC teams and briefings given by the senior management to families and survivors, but their initial duties are to make sure the flow of authentic and truthful information is pushed from the airline to handle the narrative that some social media platforms may be creating.

In an era of *'fake news'* where trust in organisations and authorities is diminished, it is vital that the airline is seen as offering confirmed, authentic and truthful information. Not speculation or conspiracy theories, but only what they know to be true. This can be challenging in a world where often the first place people will look for news is social media. Having a presence and *'pushing'* confirmed notifications can help to balance this.

To help ensure authentic communication from the airline crisis, comms teams often secure *'hashtags'* to help with searches and keywords. An example might be #ABC123 (links to the example being used in this book). The hashtags can be given out in tweets, social media posts and press statements to *'direct'* people to specific posts, knowing they are from the airline and not created by other sources.

Internal Communications

As well as external communications, handling the crisis comms internally is equally as important. Both for authentic messages to potentially traumatised colleagues and also to minimise the vacuum of information to staff. Again, this templated initial email statement can be pre-written with gaps to add when the details are available at activation. It is crucial that staff are kept informed of the actions of the different teams involved and the progress of the operation.

The internal communications can also include HR messages to support staff through counselling sessions, how to contact their manager for support (as examples) and to try and minimise the potential for staff to talk to the media. This means that it is understood that any internal communication could be leaked to the media at any time and needs sensitive handling. No information sent internally must be more detailed than the communication released to the public.

An example of an internal email can be found at the end of this chapter.

Press Conferences

There is a requirement for a senior member of the airline management team to give a press conference early on in the operation (within three hours). This will be *'live'*, meaning whoever is *'nominated'* for the role needs to know what they can say, what they cannot say, how to communicate clearly and compassionately and also offer true, open and honest information. They need to be authentic.

After offering a fuller statement with information and details that can be confirmed and read out to the media to ensure accuracy, the spokesperson should offer an apology, which is an expectation of those watching the conference. It is not an acceptance of blame, and some CEOs do find this a challenge to do, but really, it manages the expectations of those watching and the families of those who have died. It is an apology that their loved ones have been involved in the accident and that the families have been impacted.

Once key facts have been established, it is normal for the spokesperson to take questions from the media. This is the element that needs to have been practiced beforehand to know when to offer information and when to wait until it has been confirmed and get drawn into speculation. If handled well, a press conference can increase the watching public's trust in how the airline is handling the accident. If handled badly, it can increase the urge of the watching public to search for and believe in '*fake news*'.

 Tip

Watch news conferences on TV news channels, and you will observe the structure of them. The initial statement, apology and then additional information followed by questions. This set process is used for most crises, even at a low level of impact.

Media

It is vital to remember that the media have a job to do, and that job is to inform the public about the accident and offer ways of communicating with their audiences through the '*ticker tape breaking news*' approach adopted by most of the major news channels. In crisis comms, the relationship with the media, be it written or TV, needs to be as mutually beneficial as possible. This is so airlines, authorities, investigators, etc., can '*push*' news, updates, requests for information, etc., through those channels to as many people as possible. It is not enough to rely on social media platforms only.

The challenge is that media also have to have a story to offer their readership or viewers, and sometimes this can cause challenges within that relationship. Indeed, as Arokiasamy, Kwaider & Balaraman (2019) suggest, the media will look for a story, and this can lead to conspiracy theories and angles to a story to add '*drama*' to the event, not that an airline accident needs added drama. How airlines come through the response is often reliant on the success of the crisis comms process.

Sometimes, TV news channels will rely on '*experts*' to bring their views and hypotheses of an accident to speed up the storytelling and keep the pace needed to engage viewers. This can lead to what Coombs (2010) called the '*rhetorical arena*' where there are so many voices (outside the airline) that knowing where the facts of the accident lie can become difficult as each group has its own perspective on the story being told and searches out media and social platforms to reinforce the perspective they want to hear or read. This can be frustrating for the airline as they cannot compete (and should not) with the '*storytelling*' direction that the media may go in. The airline must stick to authentic, confirmed and factual information to ensure they are trusted by the families and survivors of the accident. This is a slower process than the media, and sometimes airlines are criticised for not being '*fast enough*' with the facts, but it is essential that only confirmed and real data is shared for accuracy and authenticity.

At the beginning of an accident, alongside the Telephone Enquiry Centre (TEC) being activated, there will be a media centre where callers from media outlets can get the latest statement and an update on the facts known so far. This might include registration of aircraft, type of aircraft and destination, etc., everything that would probably be in the public domain very quickly anyway. Any calls to the TEC from media will automatically be diverted to the media centre if the trained responder thinks the caller might be a journalist who is not totally open about why they are calling (see Chapter 2).

During the response, the media will be given any updated statements only after the families have been told of progress, positive identifications and updates in the family briefings at the HAC. Due to the speed of social media platforms and the fact that families and survivors often update via their own pages or use '*tweets*', this can cause some friction as it's often '*old news*' by the time journalists receive the statements. Case study 5 illustrates how a crisis comms plan that is understood and executed correctly can support how the accident operations is viewed by the public.

Case Study 5 – US 1549

In terms of crisis comms and reaction to the accident, this is a good example of having a well-thought-through plan where everyone understood their role and the importance of acting quickly.

After an emergency landing by US1549 on the Hudson River, the airline website was updated within 30 minutes, and within that timeframe, they had also released their first statement to the media. The first news release was within 45 minutes, and the CEO held his first press conference within 90 minutes. These are all within the Family Assistance Act (1996/2000) and IATA guide (2018), but to actually make them happen requires a good understanding by the crisis team and senior leadership of how to act, what to release and when to release it.

US Airways then went on to release regular updates to the media as they obtained new information. The Corporate Communication Team (internal) worked with their Marketing team to manage the main social media platforms at the time, 'Google'® and 'Yahoo!'®, to buy the keywords and terms quickly, i.e., 'Flight 1549', 'emergency landing', etc., so they could direct those who had searched these terms to the airline website, which was dedicated to the accident.

Adjusting Messages for Sales and Marketing Purposes

Having a sales and marketing colleague as part of the CMC team is vital for them to understand how they can support an operation with an adjustment to any key sales or marketing messages that may be being sent to customers. This works alongside the dark site so that not only are interactive pages in the website '*turned down*', but so are promotions. An example might be being able to stop email offers from being sent to the email list about the flight or destination or where an accident has happened. Another may be reviewing marketing promotions and slogans so as not to cause offence to those involved, however unintended. The crisis comms for sales and marketing should be the best possible and react quickly. It should also be rehearsed and trained within those teams so that everyone knows their role and is confident in achieving it, but all the positive comms can be spoiled by one unfortunate email campaign or promotion.

Case Study 6 – Reflections of an Experienced Crisis Communications Professional

Note the interviewee deployed on behalf of a Third Party Provider.

This short extract was with a Public Relations and Crisis Communication expert with over twenty years experience attending various aviation and other high-profile events both as a consultant and on behalf of a TPP.

What is the purpose of having crisis comms? And I am talking aviation here, purely aviation. Why would an airline need crisis comms? Why couldn't they do it, just do it themselves at the time of deployment?

The answer is that in the best situation, they should be able to do it themselves; in the best situation, they will have all the planning they need and they'll have all the people they need

Often, airlines believe they don't need crisis comms. They think, '*We're never going to experience this. We've got a shiny new airline with brand new 737's and new young pilots*', but of course, sometimes they do.

Do you have an example of being activated for an airline incident?

I got the call about 2:00 in the morning. The press office manager got the call probably 20 minutes, half an hour earlier, and he knew people on the plane, and he was traumatised by it, but he went through what we had exercised. We had done this so many times and gone through the different stages. He just followed the checklist of the things that he had to do, and we got the statement out. We reacted as we should, swiftly for everything. From a crisis comms point of view, it was up and running. People were contacted. Everything happened. It was very professional. To see a plan put into action in reality, not just an exercise, this just underlines the need for the preparation part of it. It worked because of the relationship that had built up over years of training and exercising.

Crisis comms act as a 'critical friend', and if the senior team doesn't have that, it can be very difficult. You have to put in the preparation, hoping you never need to use it. If you have that preparation, then it really, really works.

What do you mean by critical friend?

We need to remember that nine times out of ten, the people dealing with the accident will know people on board or they will feel it deeply. Having somebody that's a little bit more objective that can just come in, that they know and have trained with, really helps. We know what needs to be done. We can help them; we can say '*you know what to do, just put one foot in front of the other, get your templates, get your statements out*'. If they didn't have crisis comms and they had to rely internally to do it would be a lot worse because they're just traumatised. One client I worked with was so traumatised by the incident that he left the airline not long afterwards, within three months, because airlines are a close community.

Post 24-hours Crisis Communications

A lot of the crisis comms is undertaken in the first 24 hours, but maintaining regular updates continues well into the operation. Ensuring updates from the family briefings are released to the media, regular press conferences, regular videos on YouTube® and '*tweets*'. The internal emails to colleagues need to reflect the updates so staff do not feel they are being left out. Links to all press releases and videos can be included.

Collating data from social media for posts, themes, '*hits*', etc. can help build a picture of how the airline is doing in this regard. Addressing concerns raised on social media and ensuring the accuracy of information is a longer-term part of the crisis comms team.

Finally, working with the TPP (if a separate organisation) and slowly bringing back the '*functionality*' of the '*dark site*' and deciding when to revert back to the original branding colours is part of the discussions that the airline and crisis comms teams can work through. Going back too quickly may undo any of the positive messaging that has gone before. A stepped approach is more usual so that people get used to each step before undertaking the next.

Conclusions

Crisis comms is a vital part of an airline accident response. It has to support both the external messages being given to the survivors, families, media and watching public and the internal messages being given to staff and stakeholders.

The expectations of the families have risen now to a level where quick information is available to them, and they do not want to wait for news from the airline. This is understandable, but it often takes time for confirmation of facts, so the delays can cause a potential conflict with families.

The rise in social media also means the increase in '*fake news*'. The airline must always be the one known authentic voice that can be trusted to give accurate and honest updates. Without this, the watching public will turn to social media platforms to seek updates that may not always be positive for the reputation and brand of the airline.

Key Points from this Chapter

- Crisis comms is a vital part of any airline crisis, be it small- or large-scale
- Much of the initial templates for '*tweets*', website and social media posts and media statements can be pre-written and ready to be populated at the time. By doing this, they can be checked by the airline's legal department and verified ready for use
- Securing a '*hashtag*' can aid accurate and confirmed information for those who need to know. It can also help to reduce '*fake news*' by offering a guarantee of authenticity
- Having the first '*tweet*' ready to be posted within 15 minutes of notification is a challenge given the pressures of an initial phase of response. By having it templated this can be achieved
- The dark site is something that needs to be created before an accident to include agreed fonts, colours and branding. This can then be '*brought forward*' when needed and can help reduce '*interaction*' with the site but instead direct people to the contact details needed for more information

Exercise

You are part of an airline crisis comms internal team. You have been asked to consider what key information should be included in a first and then second social media post (not Twitter/X®, i.e., Facebook/Meta®, Instagram®, etc.). You have more words to enable you to create the best possible post, as you are not confined by the word limit of Twitter/X® (no photos at this stage).

Task – Think about what you would include and how you would write it, and have a go at writing one for yourself. Remember who your audience is and that the flight covers two continents and different cultures. The information on the flight follows:

Airline – ABC Airlines. Based in Hungary
Flight number – ABC123
Origin of flight – Budapest
Destination – Luton
Crash location – just outside Paris in a small village called St. Philip de Coeur (imaginary)
Passengers on board (POB) – 145 total, including 4 children
Crew number – 5
Aircraft type – Boeing 737–800
Aircraft Reg – Z-PLKC1
Captain's name – Captain James Leyton. Hours flown cannot be confirmed at this time
Last time aircraft in hangar – cannot be confirmed at this time

Templated internal email to staff (ensure they are numbered and dated for records).

Note – if possible, personalise with names

Dear colleague,

You may be aware in the news that we are currently responding to an accident. The Crisis Management Centre is open, and our crisis team is dealing with the initial activation. Some of your colleagues have deployed to (location) to support those impacted by the accident of ABC123, registration (complete) that departed from (location) to (location) on (date).

We know you will be concerned by the news, and as soon as we can update you with more information, we will. Please be assured we are doing everything possible to support those involved, and we want to support you as well. Your line manager is aware of the situation and will be contacting you shortly. HR is available in the Headquarters (location) in the foyer from 0700–2000 for the next five days to help you with any concerns or questions you may have.

There is also a newly created email for you to use for questions and concerns. The address is (add here), along with a phone number to call (add here). These are available to you 24 hours a day until further notice.

We are aware that there will be distressing footage and press coverage of the accident, and we would urge you to come forward for support as we move into the recovery phase of the accident. We would also ask you not to offer statements to the press, post about the accident on social media and if asked by media to comment, please contact HR at the email address above.

Yours (as appropriate)

Second Tweet (within 60 minutes of notification)

ABC Airlines can confirm that one of their flights (flight number) from (location) to (location) on (date) has crashed in (location). Emergency services are currently at the scene, and we have opened a toll-free number for anyone concerned about a loved one or friend. The number is (add here). Our thoughts and prayers (as appropriate) go to everyone involved, and we will be updating via this platform and the website as soon as we have more information.

First Press Statement (+60 minutes from notification)

ABC Airlines can confirm that flight no. ABC123 from (location) to (location) has crashed at (location). We can confirm the following information:

The aircraft was a (type) and the registration was (registration). There were (numbers on board) and (crew on board), but we are currently working to confirm the details of passenger names and status against our passenger manifest (as appropriate).

Emergency services are at the scene, and the NTSB are currently on their way to the crash site in (location) to begin their investigations.

Our thoughts and prayers are with everyone involved (as appropriate), and we will be cooperating with the NTSB.

ABC Airlines will also be updating information via our Twitter/X® account (add here) and our website (add address here). We also have a social media tag (add #ABC123 or similar here).

Second Press Statement

ABC airlines can confirm that one of our aircraft has been involved in an accident. Flight no. (here) from (location) to (location) with registration (registration). The accident was located in (here) at (time). There were (number) passengers and (number) crew on board.

We are deeply sorry (or as appropriate) to inform you that there have been a number of fatalities on board. Emergency services are attending, and the injured have been transferred to local hospitals. The telephone call centre is open for concerned friends and relatives to call. The toll-free number is (add here).

We will release further details as they can be confirmed. Our CEO (name) has offered his/her deepest condolences: '*Everyone at ABC Airlines is deeply shocked by what has happened today, and I wish to send my thoughts and prayers to everyone involved as well as family and friends (as appropriate). We are cooperating fully with the NTSB, and as soon as we are able, we will update everyone*'.

For our media colleagues, please do not call the toll-free number as this is a dedicated line for friends and family of those involved. Instead, please call (add here), which is the media call centre for questions and statement updates.

ABC Airlines will also be updating information via our Twitter/X® account (add here) and our website (add address here). We also have a social media tag (add #ABC123 or similar here).

Notes

1 No. 3 as of June 2023. www.similarweb.com/top-websites/computers-electronics-and-technology/social-networks-and-online-communities/
2 IATA – The International Air Transport Association. A trade association representing the world's airlines. Covers 83% of air traffic.

References and Additional Reading

Arokiasamy, L., Kwaider, S., & Balaraman, R. A. (2019). Best Practices for Crisis Communication: A Qualitative Study. *Global Business and Management Research: An International Journal*, 11 (2) pp. 141–150.

Chandler, R. C. (2010). *The Six Stages of Crisis*. s.l.: Everbridge.

Coombs, W. T. (2010). Parameters for Crisis Communication. In W. T. Coombs & S. J. Holladay (Eds.). *The Handbook of Crisis Communication* (pp. 17–53). Oxford, UK: Blackwell Publishing Ltd.

Hansson, A., & Vikstrom, T. (2011). *Successful Crisis Management in the Airline Industry: A Quest for Legitimacy Through Communication*? Florida: UPPSALA University.

IATA. (2018). *Crisis Communication and Reputation Management in the Digital Age: A Guide to Best Practice for the Aviation Industry*. (Online). Available at: www.iata.org/contentassets/86b7f57b7f7f48cf9a0adb3854c4b331/social-media-crisis-communications-guidelines.pdf.

Tullett-Prado, D., Stavropoulos, V., Gomez, R., & Doley, J. (2023). Social Media Use and Abuse: Different Profiles of Users and Their Associations with Addictive Behaviours. *Addict Behaviour*. https://doi.org/10.1016/j.abrep.2023.100479.

9 Supporting Families at the Humanitarian Assistance Centre

Chapter Objectives

By the end of this chapter, you will be able to:

- Discuss the impact that grief has on families and survivors as a way to understand the work of Special Assistance Teams (SATs) at the Humanitarian Assistance Centre (HAC)
- Describe how grief may manifest itself for families that SAT members are supporting
- Explain why the one-year memorial is key to the grief journey
- Understand how grief can also impact SAT members when leaving a deployment

Opening Quiz

1. As a SAT member, why is it important to understand how humans grieve?
2. How can knowing this help with supporting families who attend the HAC?
3. What are the main religions of the world (by numbers?)
4. How is understanding grief important for returning home as a SAT?

Glossary for this Chapter

HAC Humanitarian Assistance Centre
ICE Institute of Continued Education
SAT Special Assistance Centre

Chapter Introduction

No one human being's grief journey is the same. It is unique. There are several stages of grief, and SAT members will observe families and survivors who manifest behaviours and symptoms of grief whilst working at the HAC. It is important that SAT members understand why the families they are supporting may behave in ways that seem unusual. They should also be aware of how they can support the families they serve at the HAC or in their own homes. This chapter also helps them understand some of the reactions they may experience themselves, especially when they leave the HAC to come home. Figure 9.1 illustrates the key stages of an airline accident response and tracks it against the progression of grief to show how challenging it can be to balance the needs of the families at the HAC with the investigation and how to support them by the SAT members.

DOI: 10.4324/9781003405337-12

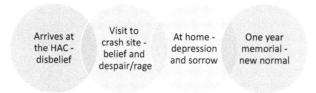

Figure 9.1 Loose linear tracking of grief with key stages of accident response

People travel through grief in their own time. There is no set timeframe, and grief can be rapid in terms of rationale and journey. It might be very slow, and sometimes people cycle around to start again when a significant date triggers their feelings of loss. Occasionally, people get *'stuck'* in grief and need clinical help to help them work through it. This chapter is not a detailed evaluation of grief but is offered as an introduction for the less experienced in this area.

Training Teams to Support Families in Distress

Many airlines train their volunteer SAT teams using standard grief models to help them understand what to expect in themselves and others to help them recognise behaviours whilst supporting the families at the HAC. As the HAC is open for a temporary and short-term timeline, it is highly unlikely that SAT members will come up against behaviours beyond the initial stages, but depending on their role post-accident, e.g., longer-term support team or the memorial team, an understanding of the full grief journey is essential.

SAT members may also experience elements of grief post-accident when returning home, and therefore, knowing how grief can impact humans is vital for their recovery and transition back into the workplace with a sense of *'post-traumatic growth'* (see Chapter 5).

Reality of the Situation

Many people find the actual process of accepting that their loved one has died in such tragic circumstances difficult. This is often the most familiar manifestation of grief that will appear at the HAC. Families arrive believing there might have been a mistake, that their loved one cannot possibly have died, and this can sometimes be misinterpreted by those supporting families. This protective response can appear to be unusual because the family has come to the HAC, so surely they must understand why they have come. Rationally, of course, families understand why they are there but might not yet be in a psychological position to absorb the enormity of the situation in which they find themselves. They may consider that their loved one might come through the front door at any moment. There is a duality here in that grieving relatives cognitively understand their loved ones are dead and will not be coming home, but their brain, in order to protect them, cannot process the information, and it is too much for them to physically, emotionally and psychologically bear.

This invisible and psychological barrier protects them from the pain of the loss. Those working with families at the HAC need to be aware of the contradictions this may present. Often, families are able to have conversations about the disposition of their loved one's remains whilst talking about their loved one in the present tense. An example sometimes seen at the HAC is a belief that their loved one managed to escape the aircraft on landing and is waiting to be found. This is why crash site visits can be so powerful for families. This is often the exact point that the inability to believe the reality of the situation transitions into them being angry with the airline,

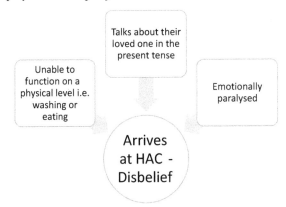

Figure 9.2 Disbelief and how it may manifest at the HAC

investigation teams, the SAT member or anyone else that they may come into contact with at the HAC as they can see their loved one has not survived the crash. This is why having professional mental health counsellors and clinicians go to the crash site visit is vital, as it can be an overpowering and physical reaction to the sight of the wreckage. Disbelief can be common for traumatised families arriving at the HAC. Figure 9.2 shows how this can potentially, physically, and emotionally manifest whilst they are there.

 Observation

Having undertaken dozens of crash site visits, this is not an uncommon reaction. However, if the crash site cannot be visited, e.g., it is at sea or a remote area, this is less common. It appears that actually seeing the crash site can be a *'reality'* moment for the families who now fully understand and can interact with what has happened.

One of the most important actions that an SAT member can undertake during this first phase of grief is to understand this contradiction of behaviours and thoughts by gently ensuring a structure is in place, which helps offer a form of stability for those who might be in a form of emotional paralysis. Basic examples of help include eating, drinking enough water, going with them to meetings and interviews and taking away any additional stress around ordering taxis, etc. What can be a surprise to less experienced SAT members is that families grieving may not display what some societies may consider *'normal'* manifestations of grief, for example, by not crying, being in control of their behaviours and being able to function as required in what appears to be a conventional way. This is the brain's way of protecting the individual from the pain, but may appear to be distressing to those observing from the outside. The key here is not to judge or try to make them understand the severity of the situation. They must do that for themselves, and the role of the SAT member is to support them when they do.

One key learning point for SAT members is not to correct the families. Telling them that *'no one survived, so their loved must be dead'* is not helpful, and individuals must transition out of this themselves, not be pushed into reality. SAT members need to remember their role is to serve and support families, not act as counsellors. There is clinical help available at the HAC, and any

SAT member that feels their family might be exhibiting extreme behaviours can go and talk to them about getting help for them.

This first phase of disbelief may not last long for families or survivors at the HAC. Being surrounded by the daily briefing, giving updates about the investigation and having positive identifications almost daily for families around them often has the effect of moving them into the second phase, where being angry at those around them takes over.

The first phase can have a physical impact on individuals. SAT members should be aware of this and look out for complaints of headaches and upset stomachs, which often accompany the first phase. It takes a lot of physical and emotional strength to psychologically protect them, and it can manifest in small aches and pains, digestive issues and headaches. One way a SAT member can really help here is to listen to stories of their loved ones in the present tense and not correct them. This is a physically demanding part of grief, and even getting up, showering, dressing and making it through the day step by step is something to be acknowledged. This is the most important part of being an SAT member, and it's something that can be taught so they understand the enormous positive impact they are having on purely helping them get through each day. It feels inconsequential, but without it, the families and survivors can feel overwhelmed and become quite unwell, needing clinical intervention.

The family briefings help offer a structure to the day alongside the meetings with the investigator and authorities. That is one of the reasons they are timed to be at the same time each day to offer the framework for stability (see Chapter 5).

The transition into feelings of despair, anger and sometimes open rage is much more challenging to support as an SAT member. These changes in how an individual might behave potentially happen once a positive identification has taken place or after a visit to the crash site so those involved understand at a fundamental level their loved ones are never going to come back through the front door again and the reality of what they are experiencing hits home.

How Families Transition at the Humanitarian Assistance Centre

This can be challenging because once an individual rationally understands that their loved one is not returning back to them, it can throw up emotions and behaviours that may not, to the outside observer, i.e., SAT member, be logical or rational in their approach. The feelings of despair and rage can be directed outwards or inwards. Outwards at the person who has died for leaving them alone, for the life that was planned and cannot be fulfilled or for the financial problems that their loss may bring. Inwards, for the guilt of feeling these emotions, for being left alone and feeling unable to cope with what life may throw at them in the future. They might also feel guilt that they were not able to stop this from happening. Why didn't they stop them from leaving on that business trip or holiday?

As stated at the beginning of this section, these behaviours and feelings are not logical but are always valid to the individual feeling them. How this stage often manifests can be confusing for both the person experiencing them and those supporting them. It is important for the SAT member to understand the families who feel this despair or rage. Their emotions and behaviours only come to the surface once they fully understand that their loved one has died and the psychological protective barrier has been lifted from them. The family may feel safer at the HAC and in the supportive environment of the SATs and those who are helping them to allow these emotions to surface. The relatives can probably shower and dress themselves without being gently nudged to do so, and a basic functioning level has been achieved. Their grief is changing.

Unfortunately, it might be the SAT member supporting them that is on the receiving end of some of the more negative behaviours and responses. A well-trained and emotionally intelligent

SAT member will be aware of this and be able to cope with what can feel quite personal. It is essential that those working at the HAC are emotionally resilient and able to accommodate the anger and remain calm and balanced in their approach.

 Tip

If the SAT member is deeply impacted by the responses to despair that may be manifesting and is distressed, it is best to remove them from the operation and send them home. The individual needs to be handled with sensitivity and gentleness, and it should be explained that this is NOT a reflection on them or how they performed. They did not fail. Instead, this is not uncommon, especially for those who have not witnessed this type of grief behaviour before, and it is about a '*duty of care*' for anyone who volunteers to step up for the role of a SAT. Ongoing support when they get home is essential to ensure they can decompress and move on from the deployment in a positive and healthy way.

This distress and despair felt by individuals experiencing grief can emerge time and again at various points during the rest of the individual's life. Weddings, holidays, birthdays and important family events can trigger the rage and can manifest again and again over the years. Transitioning through grief is rarely truly linear but for families of airline accident victims it can be especially challenging once the reality of the situation has set as Figure 9.3 reveals. SAT members cannot and should not try to fix this, make it better or move them through this part of their grief journey. Many people feel uncomfortable with seeing these types of behaviour as it is often not something that society accepts. It is something, especially in a Western society, that people tend to associate with not being in control or they can be embarrassed by it, especially if it is considered '*out of character*'. If someone we know and love is exhibiting behaviour that we haven't seen before, it can change our relationship with them for the long term. However, it is incredibly normal to feel this, and as long as it does not escalate into violence, it is something that any experienced SAT member will admit they have witnessed many times. It is important to understand it is not personal; it is not about the SAT member, rather, it is an individual, deep pain that manifests itself in these behaviours. If the first response of disbelief that their loved one has died is about feeling '*out of control*', then the transition into the despair of loss is definitely

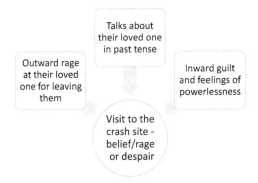

Figure 9.3 Transitioning into the next phase of grief after reality is established

more about feeling a *'focused anger'*, but it is not quick to move through this phase, and it cannot be rushed. It is also culturally and religiously divergent, dependent on demographics, the relationship with the person who has died, ethics, morals and social demands.

Feeling Let Down by Losing a Loved One

At the HAC SAT, members will not often be deployed long enough to witness the phases that follow the first two, as disbelief and despair are the most common behaviours and feelings. Often, the HAC is closed, and everyone has left when the families and survivors start to move through their grief journey at home, but it is important to understand this next phase of grief to be a professional SAT member. As part of the longer-term support team or the memorial team, understanding the full grief journey can be witnessed and should be understood.

In society, we often feel that if we keep our end of the deal with whatever Deity or belief system is in place to work hard, be kind, undertake voluntary work and give to charity, etc., we will, in some sense, be excused from trauma and tragedy. The same can happen with our health. If we give up alcohol and meat, eat plenty of vegetables and go to the gym three times a week, we will *'dodge the bullet'* of ill health. Rationally, we all understand none of this is true, but it is still somewhat of a shock if and when our health or the death of a loved one catches up with us because *'we kept our end of the deal, so what went wrong?'*

Constant thoughts around trying to deal with the loss and its impact on the rest of the individual's life are associated with feelings of guilt, the *'if only I had . . .'* thoughts and ruminations that crop up late at night or keep people awake. Going over times when we had not behaved as well as we could have done, been unkind when we could have chosen to be kind, etc. It potentially keeps us in the past and can be excruciatingly painful. It also means people can skip backwards and forwards between the feelings of despair and rage and then the impact of loss for a long period of time. If that is the case, then counselling can be helpful in breaking the cycle of regret and self-blame. It is not, however, something that can be started at the HAC or attempted, even by a mental health team whilst there. It is a long-term counsellor/client relationship, so the only support that can be offered at the HAC is for the mental health professionals or clinicians to refer someone to their local medical doctor or other appropriate help that can reach out when people go home and organise the support that is needed.

This can be the mistake that well-intentioned SAT members must overcome and resist. It is often obvious to those standing outside the situation to see the flipping between despair and the impact of their loss. The distress it can cause for individuals experiencing it and for those supporting families and wanting to help. It is important to remember that no long-term counselling should be started at the HAC that cannot be carried on after they leave. It could even make the situation worse and leave people feeling rejected and traumatised all over again.

Resist the urge to *'make them see sense'*. That is not the role of a SAT member and crosses the line of the professional relationship. This is why it is trained that SAT members should understand that their role is as a support at the HAC and not try to become their *'new best friend'*. The boundaries must be observed, and the counselling and therapy left to those whose job it is to help on their return home (see Chapter 5).

Debilitating Sorrow – at our Lowest Point

Often a confusing period, as it feels counter-intuitive for the feelings of trying to understand how the loss of their loved one impacts their lives to be at the deepest part of the grief journey when this often happens awhile after the event. However, people can transition back to despair and into feelings of debilitating sorrow and can be diagnosed with depression at any point during the grief journey. This can last for many years, depending on the individual and their relationship with the person who died.

A classic example of this is Queen Victoria, who was the Queen of Great Britain from 1837–1901. She lost her husband, Prince Albert, in 1861 and never really came through this part of her grieving process. She remained at her lowest point of grief, feeling sorrow until her death in 1901. The first two phases of grief that people transition through are often founded in the present (despair and rage) to the past (feelings of the impact of loss). Diagnosed depression, however, is very much in the present. It feels dark, painful, often physically so, and confusing. Although unique, grief can have many layers and Figure 9.4 illustrates how it can look and feel at the lowest point of grief for some people.

It is imperative at this point to split the mental illness of depression from the grieving journey of depression. The depression that grief relates to are feelings of loss and often exhaustion. Feeling physically exhausted during grief is perfectly normal and can resemble the first few weeks in that people often need to be told to have a shower, feed themselves or go outside for a walk. They lose the structure due mainly to not wanting to be engaged with life as they understand it. The feelings of insignificance and pointlessness of life can be ever-present. The challenge here is that the feeling of depression in grief often comes quite a long time after the funerals of their loved ones when others have moved on or feel able to carry on. To be reminded that someone is still grieving and quite openly can be more than a support network can cope with. Often, this is when individuals struggling with depression from grief report losing friends or people stop calling round as they do not want to be constantly reminded of death and loss. It is, however, a crucial time when individuals need that network to pull them through this, and without it, people can languish here, withdrawing from everyday life and feeling more and more isolated.

Well-meaning friends and relatives can try to pull their loved one through depression because of grief by pushing them to go out, see people, go back to work, etc. It can feel bullying, and although it is often done from love, it can have the opposite effect. Trying to get someone to ignore their grief or be distracted from it by finding a new hobby or taking up running (for example) can offer a temporary break from the feelings, but it will not take it away, and it will always return.

Professional mental health counsellors often find clients come many years after their loved one has died and find themselves only now going through the full grief journey. They have held it back for so many years by filling every second of every day either by being a workaholic,

Figure 9.4 At our lowest point in the grief journey

taking up extreme sports and training or looking after children, so they feel exhausted when they sleep. They have, in essence, returned to the first phase of disbelief that their loved ones have died and are stuck here by trying to fill every second of every day.

Depression in grief is not optional. It cannot be avoided and will appear at some point in most people. In Western society often, depression in grief, in its many forms, is seen as something that needs a tablet to '*fix it*'. Society can sometimes consider any form of sadness to be depression and that this sadness can be cured quite simply by going to a doctor and requesting a tablet to take away the pain and feelings of loss. Yes, anti-depressants can be helpful for a short period of time to regulate sleep (structure again) and bring the individual to the point of being able to regulate their own lives and function within it, but help and support through counselling or grief support groups can help alongside professional medical help.

When dealing with client's mental health, professionals are often asked '*to just take this feeling of pain away*' or '*I don't want to feel like this anymore*'. This is completely understandable, but grief has a cycle and it takes time. It cannot be shortened or hotwired to go faster. Support, understanding, a listening ear and kindness can help, but there is no timescale for this, and it will take different lengths of time for each person going through it. As mentioned earlier, it will also depend on the person's relationship with the person who died.

Anyone in this lowest point of grief should be gently encouraged to seek medical help to ascertain the type of depression that is being experienced and ensure the right help is available to them, be it in the form of clinical help through anti-depressants and/or counselling to work through their grief.

Finding a New Normal

Finding a '*new normal*' and starting to look forwards instead of backwards often coincides with the one-year memorial. The event is mandated by the Family Assistance Act (1996/2000) and ICAO Document 9973 and is usually an event on the first anniversary of the accident. Finding a '*new normal*' is not always guaranteed as Figure 9.5 shows but most people working through the grief journey will reach a point where they can start to look forward sometimes instead of backwards but this varies in terms of timescales and intensity.

Although feelings of moving forward can be reached at any point during the year, depending on the variables discussed earlier, the memorial event itself can have an impact on people where they reflect on their year and start to accept a '*new normal*' for their lives.

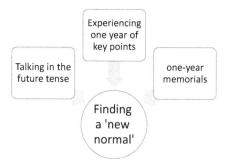

Figure 9.5 Finding a 'new normal'

However, the memorial event can have a converse impact on some people, pushing them back to feelings of despair or depression in grief due to the triggers that this can cause. An example could be going back to the HAC and the feeling this could manifest.

The HAC can be reopened for the event either at the original location or at a new one, depending on the time of year or the number of those attending. SAT members will be available to support survivors and families attending the memorial, and this is covered in more detail in Chapter 11.

One of the more positive impacts of the HAC reopening can be to allow families and SAT members to reintroduce themselves to each other, catch up on their year and have a final goodbye before separation. It also gives SAT members and all of those who have been involved in the accident response time to reflect on their roles and the event itself and spend time with the survivors or families they helped in the initial phase. Given the fast-moving response, this may be the first time that some of the teams have been able to reflect on their role, impact and reaction to the accident.

A One-Year Journey

Although the one-year memorial event is mandated by ICAO (2013), it does support learning around grief which argues that most people (not all) need a year at least to reach a point where they can start to look forward. A full year to experience the loss of their loved one through:

- Religious ceremonies or important festivals
- Birthdays
- The four seasons (or as appropriate)
- Cultural events that might have been important for the family member
- Anniversaries for couples
- Other significant events that were a custom for the family member

Going through these at least once is often essential for people to feel able to move to a '*new normal*'. They will have to '*experience*' these events without their loved one. Obviously, as discussed throughout this chapter, not everyone moving through grief will do so in a linear or clean process. People can be triggered to slip back to more painful feelings and behaviours, but the memorial event can be helpful for some of the families to revisit their time at the HAC, catch up with the SAT members that supported them and remember their loved ones when the permanent memorial is unveiled.

Supporting Religions at the Humanitarian Assistance Centre

According to ICE, the Institute for Continuing Education (part of Cambridge University),[1] the top five religions (by numbers) are as follows:

1. Judaism
2. Christianity
3. Islam
4. Hinduism
5. Buddhism

Religion may be crucial to some families at the HAC who feel they need to or wish to undertake specific rituals around death. This can be challenging given the overriding requirements of positive identification through scientific means (see Chapter 10). An example may be the rituals of cleansing and burial for loved ones of the Islamic faith. This cannot usually be undertaken at the operational mortuary as the loved one concerned could be several days/weeks from being identified.

Those working at the HAC will try very hard to accommodate the religious requirements of families, such as meeting dietary requirements, providing separate religious rooms and finding local pastoral support (if possible). Of course, not all families want or need to undertake religious rituals but may require a '*quiet space*' for reflection, and this can also be accommodated. Depending on the location, there may be certain restrictions on some faiths to openly undertake rituals, but in most countries, whatever their leading faith is usually allows other religions to mourn freely.

 Observation

In 43 deployments, I have never experienced a country ban another religion during an accident response. All have been accommodating even if the faith is completely opposite to the local one. Finding local pastoral support, however, can be much more challenging depending on where you are in the world. Building regional pastoral networks as part of the planning process can really pay dividends if needed in a real response.

When Special Assistance Team Members Leave the Humanitarian Assistance Centre

In Chapter 5, the process for SAT members handing over to a new colleague and leaving the HAC was detailed. It is important, however, to remember that everyone who works at the HAC with traumatised families in a high-pressure environment for any period of time may experience a form of grief themselves when they leave.

SAT members often report that they feel a '*loss*' when they leave the families and colleagues that they have naturally become very close to and worked together intensively over a number of weeks. They can feel conflicted as their own families and friends will miss the SAT member, and often, people report feeling '*alienated*' for a while when they return home. They may feel '*angry*' when the world has carried on without them and does not acknowledge the experience they have been through. This is perfectly normal and rarely lasts for very long. This will largely depend on the social support in place for the individual when they return home (Sanchez & Viswesvaran, 2002) and how the airline takes care of the response teams on their return.

Having a team of specialists that can support colleagues who have worked at the HAC over a longer time period can alleviate a lot of the potential challenges that post-deployment can bring. Regular catch-ups as a team to discuss how they are experiencing their transition among colleagues who may also feel the same and can understand what they have witnessed. Having individual sessions to allow everyone to understand and express their concerns can identify any colleagues who might need more intensive support.

Most people transition back to their '*normal functional*' world with no problems at all. Sleep, reconnection with family and friends and getting back to a work routine will work for most people. Having a longer-term support system can catch the small number of people who may need a little extra help to transition.

Conclusions

By understanding how grief is an individual journey taking in a variety of feelings, behaviours and reactions and by training SAT members to recognise them and feel comfortable with them, it is possible to really increase knowledge and skills for the teams working at a HAC. A good, solid understanding of the work required by SATs and what to expect from the families and survivors they may support at the HAC can help SAT members feel less anxious about supporting families who are mourning a loved one.

Human beings move through grief at very individual speeds; some slowly and perhaps never really reaching the point where they can look forward to a '*new normal*', others more quickly. All of this is largely dependent on their relationship with the person who is deceased. Additionally, the impact that the deceased has on the family left behind and cultural, social and demographic differences.

The HAC is open for the short term, usually, no longer than four to six weeks. Families come to gain information from the authorities on the investigation, offer information (DNA and interviews) and leave (hopefully) with a positive identification and their loved one repatriated home. A greater understanding of grief and how it can impact people can be a powerful tool for inexperienced SAT members to find confidence in supporting families.

Key Points from this Chapter

- Grief is an individual journey that will depend on several factors for how it will impact them and their feelings of loss
- Grief will have a different impact on an individual physically, emotionally and psychologically
- SAT members should not try to '*counsel*' at the HAC. This should be left to the mental health professionals who can support individuals by '*referring*' them
- Given the timescales, it is likely that the families will probably only manifest the early phases of grief, such as '*disbelief that their loved one has died*' and '*despair about the impact that their loved one's loss will have on them*' but it is imperative that SAT members understand grief and the impact it can have on people to be successful in their role
- The one-year anniversary is mandated by legislation but can also act as a marker point after a full year of experiencing significant family or personal events, i.e., birthdays
- Understanding grief as a topic is useful for SAT members to understand as they may experience it themselves when they get home whilst transitioning from the HAC to their home life and workplace

Quiz

Take a few minutes to complete this quiz to check your understanding of this chapter.

1. Why is it important to support a daily structure when families first arrive at the HAC?
2. How can a SAT member help support practical structure for grieving families at the HAC?
3. Why is it important that SAT members should not counsel the families they are supporting?
4. Who can help families at the HAC access support when they leave?
5. Why is the family briefing so important? And why is it held at the same time every day?
6. Why is the crash site visit vital for families who may be struggling to believe their loved one has died?
7. Name three significant markers that people usually have to experience in the first year of losing a loved one.

Note

1 ICE – Institute for Continuing Education. Part of Cambridge University.

References and Additional Reading

Family Assistance Act. (1996/2000). (Online). Available at: www.ntsb.gov/tda/er/Pages/tda-fa-aviation. aspx.

ICAO. (2013). *Assistance to Aircraft Accident Victims and Families, Doc 9998/499*. Montreal: International Civil Aviation Organization.

Sanchez, J. I., & Viswesvaran, C. (2002). The Effects of Temporal Separation on the Relationships Between Self-Reported Stressor at Work. *Organizational Research Methods*, 5 (2) pp. 173–183.

10 Search and Recovery, Identification, Repatriation and Personal Effects

Chapter Objectives

By the end of this chapter, you will be able to:

- Explain how a crash site is gridded and human remains recorded
- Describe how the deceased are positively identified
- Explain what the repatriation team does
- Understand the decisions that have to be made by families regarding their loved ones
- Describe the two '*categories*' for personal effects
- Explain how items are catalogued for families to claim

Opening Quiz

1. Why is it important to understand other areas of an accident operation away from the HAC?
2. Why bother gridding and using flags to mark '*items of interest*' at the crash site?
3. Can identification take place by visual approval?
4. Do search and recovery teams gather and record personal effects or just those items of value, i.e., laptops?

Glossary for this Chapter

DNA Deoxyribonucleic acid
DVI Disaster Victim Identification
HAC Humanitarian Assistance Centre
SAT Special Assistance Team
SID Senior Incident Director

Chapter Introduction

Whilst the Humanitarian Assistance Centre (HAC) is open and supporting survivors and families, as well as bringing together the authorities and agencies central to a response of this kind, the work of the search and recovery teams will be ongoing at the crash site. This chapter will give an introduction to the work that the various teams do for search and recovery, identification,

DOI: 10.4324/9781003405337-13

repatriation and personal effects. It is important to understand what other processes are being followed alongside the HAC as it does impact decisions made there. However, this chapter will not go into the forensic details of the accident response.

There are various teams that sit within the operation of identifying the deceased as well as returning them to their loved ones. They range from the national government of the location of the site, investigation teams, recovery teams that are equipped and trained to recover human remains and teams to recover personal effects, all working together to ensure a cross-referenced, mapped and sensitively searched crash site.

For the purposes of this chapter, we will be concentrating on search and recovery in the main, but the range of teams will always answer directly to the investigation teams and especially the Senior Incident Director (SID) in charge. No one can enter or leave the crash site without their permission, and communication is vital to ensure the work on the site is undertaken to the very best standards required by ICAO Annex 13 (2021) and Annex 9 (2013).

Some of the Go Team that might have deployed initially and worked to support the organisation or at the airport could, if their skills and qualifications allow, switch over to the search and recovery teams once permission is given to enter the site. This is only given once the last of the survivors have been extracted, and there is no chance of anyone being alive there anymore.

Gridding the Site

Before gridding takes place, pictures are taken of everything *'in situ'*.

Gridding is the ability to ensure everything found at a crash site is flagged (literally a small flag placed at the precise location), recorded and mapped so an overall view of a crash site can be established for all of the teams working there, but ultimately the investigation team.

Initially, a full search will take place in a gridding formation where the whole site will be plotted, either manually (depending on location and terrain) or, more likely today, completed by a drone. Each team will then undertake a painstaking search of a given grid location using specific coloured tags to identify the following:

- Any human remains
- Personal effects
- Aircraft equipment or similar as requested by the investigation team. Examples could be the location of the black box or parts of the aircraft engine, etc.

Depending on the skills of the team, they may specialise in one area, i.e., human remains or personal effects. Each flagged find is documented, recorded, numbered and bagged before being photographed and removed to another location, such as a mortuary.

Challenges for Gridding a Site

Aircraft crash sites are, by their nature, not always in flat and easy-to-reach terrain. They can be difficult to locate and even harder to manage as a site, i.e., Germanwings[1] was in a mountainous area. This means gridding a site may have to be undertaken on multiple occasions as the site itself can move or, in poor weather, elements may move within a gridded site. That is why photographing and recording the location of findings at each step is so important. The example shown in Figure 10.1 shows the devastation of a crash site and highlights the need for gridding and photographing every section to ensure an organised and detailed record of the whole site.

Figure 10.1 Crash site of Turkish Airlines TK 1951

Interstate Aviation Committee, Public domain, via Wikimedia Commons

Wildlife can also be a challenge both for the preservation of the crash area and those who are working on it, and this adds an extra layer of security for those working on the site. There is strict legislation about shooting wildlife under any circumstances, so often, teams will take advice from the authorities and engage with wildlife experts locally to support them who understand the best ways to handle the situations before it can get out of hand.

Security itself can be a problem. Although Go Teams and authorities can be quick to arrive at a crash site, it is a possibility that local residents may enter the site before it can be secured. Either to help those who are injured or to remove items thinking they are being helpful. The quicker the site can be secured is essential to minimise the '*contamination*' of crash sites for evidence. Even moving expensive items to a secure location, such as iPads or phones or any item that contains data for the arriving investigating teams, can be a challenge as they have invariably not been photographed or recorded in location as per the gridding process, so knowing what equipment might be linked to what passenger becomes much harder.

Onlookers and media may also inadvertently and innocently '*contaminate*' a site for evidence as they try to understand and convey the seriousness of the situation. Again, having some sort of local authority take early control of security can minimise the damage caused by walking around the site and moving items especially the 'black box' as indicated in Figure 10.2. Sometimes, the location and openness of locations can add to the complexity of securing a site and ensuring all evidence and the deceased are kept '*in situ*' for recording and photographing as evidence for a future investigation and inquiry. The support of local authorities is absolutely paramount to the success of this part of the operation.

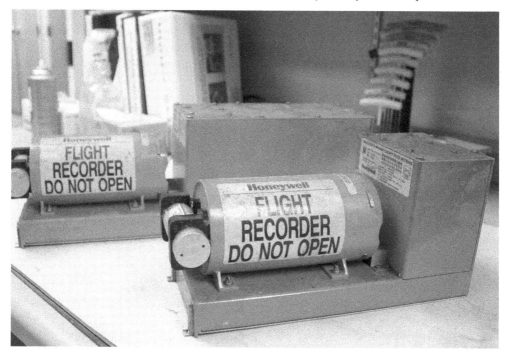

Figure 10.2 Asiana 214 black box official photo from NTSB

Reproduced courtesy of NTSB via Wikimedia Common

Human Remains Retrieval

Each individual part of human remains found on the site will be allocated a Disaster Victim Identification (DVI) number. Each item found must have a DVI form completed and finally photographed for the form at a later date. This means the site may be covered in a large number of coloured tags and accumulate a large number of forms that help in the identification process.

Each item will be placed in a specially designed pouch and can then be stretchered from the site or removed depending on size. For some locations that might involve specialist lifting equipment and teams such as mountain rescue, always remembering there is a chain of custody for everything removed from a site, from human remains to parts of the aircraft, and that wherever it is taken for further analysis, it can be located at any time by any of the teams that might need to see it or test it.

Recent media coverage of search and recovery in natural disaster situations, such as the huge earthquake in Turkey and Syria in February 2023,[2] showed the enormous task of locating human remains, and this often involves cadaver dogs who are specially trained to sniff out and locate those remains. The job can be long and tiring. It can be challenging both in terms of location, terrain and what the teams are witnessing. The priority of all the teams is to sensitively, quickly and carefully find all human remains so that a positive identification and repatriation to wherever the families wish them to be sent can be undertaken as quickly as scientifically possible.

The deceased, personal effects and equipment may have to be carried manually over distances that cranes and helicopters (for example) might not be able to access. Although the teams are all trained for such scenarios, it can be traumatic and physically exhausting to undertake such work.

Any personal effect found on the deceased will be left '*in situ*' and removed to the mortuary but may be separated at that point to be examined elsewhere. This means the paperwork needs to quickly and easily identify what items belong to each body or part recovered.

Whenever human remains are taken from the site, they are treated with the utmost care and dignity (ICAO Annex 13).

Identification

The identification of human remains takes place in a mortuary. This may be one situated nearby, depending on location or, if in a remote area, where a mortuary is not easy to come by, a temporary one may be built. This is not uncommon, and teams can be brought in to quickly build a '*flat packed*' specially-built mortuary that can be put up in quick time and removed afterwards and taken away.

Assuming a large-scale operation, the teams will include the following qualified and trained teams, all working together in a mortuary or in adjacent buildings. They are listed in no particular importance:

a. Triage – an initial team that receives the tagged and recorded remains in the mortuary and can check all the paperwork and information contained within it is correct before taking custody of it and allocating it to a further team
b. Anthropology – determine gender from bones, age, height, race, and other physical determinants
c. DNA – taking a sample of DNA to be tested against records in systems or a sample taken in the HAC by a family member for comparison (see Chapter 7)
d. Finger/Foot Printing – another means of identification through records, i.e., criminal or military
e. Odontology – identification from dental X-rays compared to records bought by families or shared upon request through a judge
f. Pathology – this is where a forensic post-mortem will take place by examining the body (or parts) to collect physical and clinical evidence to support the '*cause of death*' (College of Policing, 2019)
g. Photography – every single item that is bought into the mortuary facility is photographed again in a more clinical environment for the records and to aid further investigation
h. Radiography – X-ray or MRI scan
i. Support – A team trained to support the operation that can process photographs and files confidentially and accurately to aid a further investigation

Figure 10.3 details the transition of human remains from the crash site, transferring to the mortuary, flowing through the mortuary and then through to identification.

Remember that each team (in a large enough operation) may be allocated a '*records team*' that works cross-functionally to ensure accurate information, storage of items and easy access for the teams should that be necessary. This means teams working nearby in offices that might be supporting the mortuary teams would not necessarily be exposed to the mortuary or see human remains. The most appropriate skills in terms of administration or information logging can be utilised without causing trauma or harm to those involved. In fact, access to mortuaries is limited anyway to those people who have a job that requires them to be there. They are sterile locations with a protocol for dress, cleaning, disposal of equipment and protective clothing, and access to anyone who is not required is prohibited.

Figure 10.3 Overview of the flow of human remains from the crash site to returning to the family

Whilst all cultural and religious rites will be met if at all possible, given the nature of the operation and the investigation, it is not always possible to meet all of the requirements of the death rites for all cultures or religions. This would be explained to the families at the HAC by experienced personnel to avoid further distress.

Ante-Mortem Forms and Post-Mortem Forms

Whilst at the HAC, the families and survivors may be interviewed using a yellow INTERPOL missing person form to help establish identifiable facts about the person, such as hair colour and scars from operations, etc. This yellow form is then sent to the mortuary to help with the pink post-mortem form that concentrates on the physical identifiers helpful for positive identification. The yellow forms may record features on the deceased that the teams can identify through examination.

The information from both forms is put into a specific system used by INTERPOL, and the system picks out themes and pairings. Further filtering and funnelling of information, data and further analysis can support a positive identification. This could be by DNA, dental records and scars matched with physical evidence taken from X-rays or post-mortems.

Only once a sufficient level of confidence has been met by reconciling the two forms will the positive identification be approved by an objective and experienced panel, including the local judiciary, who review all of the presented data and then decide if the identification is met. For a positive identification to take place, there needs to be a match for dental records and/or fingerprints and a 100% match for DNA. This is supplemented by secondary information (ante-mortem) in areas such as clothing, jewellery and tattoos, etc.

This is the point that the families are told about the notification at the HAC, and decisions can be made about how they wish to proceed with their loved one's journey.

Introduction to Human Identification

In different regions of the world, the process of obtaining a positive identification varies. Some countries will allow facial recognition (if possible), but for most countries signed up to the Family Assistance Act (1996/2000), two scientific processes must be obtained and agreed to allow for positive identification as Figure 10.4 illustrates. These can include:

- Odontology from a mouth and jaw X-ray
- Fingerprints or toe prints
- DNA from a living relative – needs a 100% match, so usually taken from the maternal line

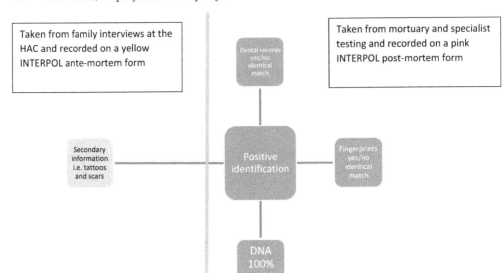

Figure 10.4 Primary and secondary identifiers for a positive identification

Table 10.1 Three scientific identification processes

Process	How obtained	Issues
DNA (mouth swab)	From a close relative (usually from the female side) obtained at the HAC or from their own home	Issues if adopted, identical twins if both are deceased. Can also depend on where taken from the deceased. Needs a 100% match
Fingerprints	Taken in the mortuary and compared to records	Not likely if the individual appears nowhere on records or does not have a copy of their fingerprints. Need to know nationality to help filter this down. Needs a Yes/No answer for a match
Odontology (mouth X-ray)	Taken in the mortuary or hospital if equipment is not available	Need something to compare to. If no family has come forward with records, this can be extremely challenging. Needs a Yes/No answer for a match

Other interesting identification information can come from product or manufacturer numbers on areas such as knee or hip replacements or breast implants, as these can be traced back to the original records and name (see Chapter 7 for details on secondary information via the INTERPOL forms). Table 10.1 indicates the three main scientific processes for identification.

This sounds straightforward and easy to obtain and test, but often, they are challenging and have to be sent to specific laboratories that are limited in number around the world. These cannot be completed on-site and in the mortuary. This takes time, and that is why often the positive identification takes so long.

Once the results are conclusive and the two INTERPOL forms (pink and yellow) are also complete and added to the results, a panel then decides on identification before the families can be told.

Notifying the Families of a Positive Identification

Often, a positive identification takes place whilst the families are still at the HAC and can be handled by the authorities, such as the prosecutor, Coroner/Medical Examiner, DVI teams or police, and with a SAT member present if they wish to support the families. Once this takes place, only then will this information be released in the daily briefing to the families as a whole by the DVI or investigation teams and then to the media. Remembering the policy is always to tell the families the key information first before releasing it at the daily briefing or to the press.

The families then have to decide, with the support of the SAT member and with help from mortuary teams, to answer the following questions:

- Do they want to repatriate their loved ones as they are now? Any further fragments of human remains will go in a memorial grave with their fellow passengers (see Chapter 11).
- Do they want to wait for more fragments of human remains to be found and delay repatriation until the response is complete?
- Do they wish to have their loved one cremated and take home their ashes instead?
- Do they want to be informed if more fragments of human remains of their loved one are subsequently found?
- Is there anything else specific to their loved one they wish the teams to observe or carry out?

As this list shows, along with Figure 10.5 the choices that have to be made by families can be arduous and traumatic. The teams at the HAC will support the families as much as possible but ultimately it is the families that must decide what options they want to take.

These are terribly hard decisions for families to make, and being at the HAC with other families making similar decisions can be a source of comfort whilst they are made. Of course, the families have to make these decisions themselves, and although help in the form of information can be given, the families are never led or guided down a certain path. Each decision must be made independently (see Chapter 7).

Once decisions have been made, the families can turn to repatriating their loved ones or undertaking whatever ritual is most appropriate for them at the time.

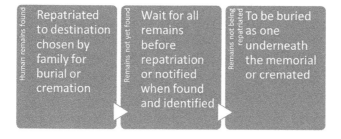

Figure 10.5 Choices made by families for their loved ones at the HAC upon a positive identification

For families who have left the HAC and gone home or did not come in the first place, the conversations are exactly the same as airlines are required to support families who stay in their homes, and the SAT members and teams will go to them.

Some families may not always get a positive identification, and again, this can depend on the location, terrain and circumstances of the incident, i.e., in the cases of MH370[3] where no bodies were found, MH17 because of the location of the crash site meant teams had a limited amount of time to locate and retrieve as many human remains as they could and where crashes occur over sea, such as AF447 over the Atlantic Ocean.[4]

Repatriation

This is a completely separate team that works in conjunction with the mortuary teams. They concentrate on the safe and accurate delivery of loved ones back to their families. They usually have an excellent working knowledge of all the regulations and laws that are linked to transporting and moving human remains safely and securely. ICAO Annex 9 details repatriations.

The teams will complete the necessary documentation to *'export'* and then *'import'* the deceased to a given destination, and this can take a while as some countries will rely on several languages of documentation being processed, signed by specific governmental departments or individuals and transported in specific coffins, or other similar storage dependent on local laws. Often, the final preparations before departure are overseen by local officials or relevant embassy representatives. This is the point when requested flags can be added to the coffins and specific prayers or ceremonies undertaken.

Families at the HAC are always told not to plan for burials for whatever religion or cultural requirement they may have until their loved one has actually been formally identified and approved to be put on an aircraft, as it can take several weeks to eventually be given permission to move someone. Also, getting loved ones on a flight that can be full can take a while. Finally, one of the greatest challenges for transporting coffins is ensuring if there is a connecting flight to smaller airports, that the coffin will fit onto the smaller aircraft as it could result in a loved one being *'stuck'* in a hub airport whilst overland arrangements are made. Part of the repatriation teams' tasks is to understand the full journey and to communicate fully with the family and the funeral home, or similar if other arrangements need to be made so everyone understands this and anticipates it.

Depending on the decisions made, families often want to have a flag to cover their loved one's coffin when it is placed on the first part of the journey, that is, as it's placed in an aircraft hold starting their final journey and when it is removed at the destination. The repatriation team will organise this if it is possible and allowed depending on the local regulations and can often gain permission to be on the apron to record the event so the family can see it has been undertaken if they cannot view this from where they are.

If families do not travel with their loved one, they may also ask for someone to accompany their loved one on the final flight home, and often SAT members will volunteer to do this, especially if they have been supporting the family at the HAC or in their homes.

Fragmented Remains that Are Not Repatriated

Some families will want to claim every single identified part of their loved one and wait for that to be complete before starting the process of repatriation and burial. Their loved ones will be held at a local funeral director. Others may want to claim the remains that were able to identify their loved one and not claim the rest so that the journey can start sooner. There is no right or wrong answer to this, and each family will do what is best for them at that time.

This does mean that usually there are additional human remains at the end of the operation, and this is where the memorial team will offer their expert help. This is discussed in Chapter 11, but suffice to say that memorials often include the additional remains of the passengers that are interred together in a specially designed storage area alongside or underneath the memorial stone or similar.

Personal Effects

As part of the recovery operation taking place in line with supporting families at the HAC, there will be a team recovering the personal effects from the site and removing them once they have been tagged, recorded and photographed.

There are two main categories of personal effects. First, there are *'associated personal effects'*. These are items found *'on'* the deceased, either as rings (for example) or wallets in pockets. Only those items that can be definitively identified as being *'on the person'* of the deceased and can, therefore, be categorised as linked to or *'associated'*. If an item is found next to someone, even if the team believes it is obvious it could only belong to them, this is not definitively attributed to them and will be referred to as *'unassociated personal effects'*.

This is the second category, and these are items that are not directly *'attributed'* to the deceased, which could include wallets found directly next to the deceased, laptop bags or shoes, etc. These have to be treated as potentially linked but not definitively and recorded accordingly.

If items are found directly on the deceased, as part of the positive identification, a discussion may be happening with the families at the HAC to decide what they would want to do with their loved one's personal effects, more importantly, how they want the items to be returned to them.

Families have several options here:

1. Sanitized only to ensure no biological hazard – returned *'as is'*, e.g., bloodstained shirt but without a biological hazard. Often, families want items back as authentic as possible when found.
2. Sanitised and cleaned – returned with as much of the bloodstain as possible removed. Never promised as 100%, but as close as possible.
3. Cleaned and restored – for jewellery only (including watches).

Again, along with choices made by families for the remains of their loved ones they must also make difficult decisions about how, or if, they want their loved ones personal effects returned to them (if found) and Figure 10.6 gives an overview of the choices available.

Most associated items are returned to the families as soon as possible after a positive identification has taken place. If the family is still at the HAC, this may take place there before they leave with their loved ones. This can be a very moving but ultimately satisfying result for the teams involved as families take great comfort in having their loved one's items returned to them.

Not all items are returned straight away. Laptops, mobile phones, iPads, etc. are usually kept as evidence as they can be crucial for the investigation, i.e., photos taken. Clearly, items of this nature may have malfunctioned or broken during the impact, and the teams in the mortuary have the skills to be able to extract information from them via the chip. The teams work hard to ensure this can be achieved not only for the investigations but also for the families. It is not always possible and takes time and lots of effort, but the teams do often achieve tremendous results.

Once the personal effects have been cleared from the crash site, they need to be housed and held whilst decisions are made on how they are returned to the family or catalogued as items are bought to a facility, usually a warehouse, as there can be many thousands of pieces of personal

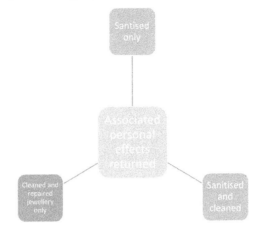

Figure 10.6 Options for the return of associated personal effects

effects to recover. This could be held and processed locally or, more likely, transferred to a specialist facility that has expert teams that can clean and repair items as well as log them.

Cataloguing Unassociated Personal Effects

Items that cannot be associated and returned to the family are recorded, photographed and recorded in both a hard copy catalogue and electronically. There are lots of systems available for this to happen, and a Third Party Provider (TPP) that has the facilities, skills and equipment to undertake this monumental task is usually retained.

Every item is saved and no judgements are made on their value, so this ranges from items of jewellery to makeup and handkerchiefs. Each is photographed, given a reference number and *'grouped'* and then inserted into the catalogue. This is then placed on the *'family website'* so that families can view the items and make a claim for them. The claim is not a guarantee of the item being returned at this stage, but many items can be returned this way.

Those items that have a high value, i.e., jewellery, and that have received several claims must go through a court process that includes families offering evidence for the items, i.e., invoices, receipts and photos of their loved one wearing the specific piece of jewellery. A court will sometimes be required to make a judgement on who will receive the item.

Items that cannot be claimed are:

- Cash – unless it came out of an associated item, e.g., a wallet
- Guns or other items of weaponry, *including* swords and ceremonial knives, etc.
- Contraband, i.e., drugs
- Liquids, sweets, perfume, pharmaceuticals – could be contaminated, so would never be given back to families even if associated

These are destroyed with witnesses from the airline, government, and other representatives from various agencies, i.e., TPP, to ensure destruction.

The catalogue is open and online for a set period of time, with the families informed through written communication when the items will be stored away and potentially destroyed. The best practice for storing items for unclaimed *'unassociated personal effects'* is 24 months, but often airlines will pay for facilities to keep them for much longer as families sometimes ask for more time to feel able to look through the catalogue.

Again, any destruction of unclaimed items over a set and agreed period of time is witnessed and recorded.

Case Study 7 – Reflections from an Experienced Mortuary Operations Professional

Note – the interviewee deployed on behalf of a Third Party Provider.

When you arrive at the crash site, what are your priorities?

Usually, the search and recovery teams are allowed onto the crash site after the investigators, authorities and the police have already been on and finished their work, and it's handed over to the airline. The investigation teams, authorities and the police have collected all the human remains and personal effects that they can find or specific aircraft parts that would support the investigation into the cause of the accident (black box). They may leave other personal effects on the site or they may be difficult to find. Our role as search and recovery, on behalf of the airline, is to collect additional human remains and personal effects to support the investigation and identification process.

We usually work alongside the wreckage salvage team, who may be collecting engine parts, etc. We have to agree on how we are going to work together. In some cases, the site may have already been gridded by the authorities or investigation team.

In some cases, the site may not have been gridded. Therefore, we will come up with a plan together on how to grid the site to help us all understand where the engine parts are picked up from, where the parts of the plane are picked up from and if we find any more personal effects or human remains to help the investigators.

So, really, it's about putting a plan together with the airline, with the wreckage salvage company and ourselves to decide how we will move forward. The end goal is clearing the site and putting it back to how it was originally.

First of all, we look at the map of what the investigators have given us for where the crash site area is, and it may be inside the airport or outside the airport, or it might be partially in both. It may have been completely out of the airport, i.e., in an urban area or rough terrain.

We will look at the size of the crash site, and then we will start gridding it in 50-metre squares until we've covered the area, or where we think the area is. Sometimes, that might have to be extended if we find things as we go along that sit 'outside' where we have gridded.

The search and recovery team usually go in first to collect any human remains and personal effects not already collected by the authorities or investigation teams. The team leaves any engine parts in situ, so our first job would be to go in with marks and flags, and the salvage team comes in after that.

We start by looking at marking our findings, such as anything to do with personal effects, anything to do with human remains, and most probably help the wreckage salvage company and the authorities mark the other pieces in situ as well if we can. We also may be tasked by the investigation team to find items that their teams didn't find, which could be very important to the investigation. So we're actually helping them as well and supporting them to find pieces that they may not have found.

We start going through that site with a team in a line, and we'll go through as much of the site as we possibly can, picking everything up and gently bagging everything in individual bags and giving them an individual number. We will keep everything separate even though we may find several items in the same place because it is important where we find it, and we will make a note of what coordinate it is and what square it was found in. The reason for the markers initially before we started was to photograph everything. It gives you a picture of the 50-metre square, and then when we start putting things into bags so, we know that if it is in A1 square (for example), we know where we picked up a certain item from, but with a photograph it will actually show you exactly where it was. This helps to cross-reference everything. Sometimes, we use GPS systems so that we can mark the piece exactly where we find it.

Everything is marked. Everything, such as the human remains or personal effects, and when the salvage company follows behind us, they will then do exactly the same, but they will mark the parts of the aircraft that they find or parts of the engine. Eventually, whatever we find from A1 and whatever the wreckage team finds from A1 gives us the best picture of the scatter pattern of where the two sets of pieces are.

Once you've done your pass, you've gridded everything and you've marked everything and all of that, then what do you do?

Before all of this started, we will have spoken to the investigators. We will have come up with a plan with them as well. It will be a case of if we find any human remains, there will be a process put in place by the investigators to show what's been found for forensic reasons for human remains, and they will be handed over to the forensic labs within whoever's looking after the identification process.

We have a process for understanding how to handle anything we find, and then they will put that into the system and continue the identification process. With regards to personal effects, depending on what we are finding, if we are finding things that include a data item, and that means anything that captures either pictures or sound, they want them as part of the investigation in case anybody heard something before the accident or took a photograph or recorded anything. So, anything to do with data writing will be automatically handed over to the investigators.

The other personal effects that we collect will then go to wherever we are allowed to start processing those. Sometimes, we process them '*in country*', and we would be given a large enough space to do that processing and logging them in a system.

We then hand the site over to the wreckage salvage company to finish their processing.

So, do you then go and work in the mortuary, or is that your job done?

That very much depends on where we are at the time. There are countries in the world where it overwhelms them, you know, because they may be used to, maybe, lots of deaths in those countries of shootings and things like that, which would become part of their usual forensic processes. But what they may not be used to is fragmented body parts, and this might overwhelm their team and potentially their systems. Therefore, we will provide them with some of our specialist forensic people to support them and help them.

In some cases, we are allowed help. In other cases, we are not, and whatever is done in the mortuaries has to be done by their forensic teams, and we just then have to wait until the outcome of the investigation by either the police team or whoever is doing it. They will then tell us if they get a positive identification.

So, how would the airline be involved in repatriation?

We would not expect the airline employees to be on the crash site and would not expect airline employees to be working in the mortuary, but we might be able to work alongside airline employees when we are processing personal effects just to give them some idea of what we are actually doing to get the end result. With regards to repatriations, the authorities are only concerned about the identification of those people who were on board. Once that is done, then their job is finished.

They will then release the remains to the airline as their responsibility is to start the repatriation process. Most airlines do not have the skill set to do the repatriations, and we would be involved in bringing in a repatriation team to gather what decisions and information we need, you know, from the families. That is normally done in interviews at the HAC, or it may be at their home if they haven't travelled to the HAC. It could be our team, or it might be the airline that gets information from those families on what their wishes would be for their loved one, whether they want them to be buried '*in country*', whether they want them to be repatriated home. Once the positive identification has taken place, they will have a lot more involvement. Everyone thinks that the authorities will do everything but only up to a certain point, and that's the identification piece.

The repatriation piece will fall on the airlines to get the information required and to action those repatriations and the wishes of the families.

This is a specialist job. It's not something that somebody could pick up as they go along. You need qualified people, and we use skilled funeral directors who understand the required documentation. They need to understand the culture of the families to carry out the funeral rites before we even start thinking about the repatriation.

How does the airline get involved in personal effects?

The airline gets involved in personal effects in a couple of ways. One, they will contract a company to be responsible for processing the personal effects, and again, that is likely to be a Third Party Provider.

As with repatriation, before you can carry out the personal effects process, you need to make sure you've involved all the families, and you need to make sure you carry out whatever wishes they want, as we are processing personal effects. The airline would work alongside us in getting that information from the families, and it could be done at the HAC, or it may be having to go to the family's home again.

We need to know if the families want to take part in that process. Some families do not want to take part in the process of personal effects. For whatever reason, they may not want anything back.

Does that mean they don't want anything back at all?

Nothing at all, even if we have associated items that we know belong to their loved one, they may not want those back for whatever reason. People have different choices, but we have got to categorise them into two sections, '*associated*' items and '*unassociated*' items. So we will involve the airline with the *'associated'* items once we have processed them; we then get the wishes of the family on how they would like them returned, whether they want them sanitised, whether they want them cleaned or whether they want them cleaned and restored and once we have those wishes, then we can go ahead and carry out those wishes. So, if it's a watch, as an example, and they want to have it cleaned and repaired, we obviously have to involve the insurance companies in this because there will be a price to do the restoration work on a watch. Normally they give us a limit to where we can spend without asking them each time, and that could be £500 an item (for example). That helps as we do not have to keep going back each time to get permission. If it was a Rolex® and it's going to cost £2,000 however, we would need to go back to the insurers for permission.

So, they just do it on a case-by-case basis, then?

It is, yes. And once we have permission, we can go ahead and clean the watch and have it restored as per the family's wishes. It's returned in a nice presentation box with packaging along with anything to be returned to the family, and the airline then has two options. The airline can use their own SAT members to deliver them to the families, but in some cases, because the airlines are so small, they would ask us to do it with our humanitarian assistance team members.

Finally, it might be a joint venture, so sometimes it may be one of them and one from our team. If it's a difficult return, i.e., a child's personal belongings, maybe we would send one of our psychologists from the airline, because we do not know what the reaction is going be of the families and we need to be there to support them.

The airline has a responsibility to store all items for a minimum of two years or whatever is agreed with the insurance companies and the families if longer.

Conclusions

The operations that take place outside the HAC and away from the families is a highly skilled and intricate one that involves the gridding, flagging and recording of every single piece of human remains and the crash site. The personal effects are then also recorded and mapped and cleaned or repaired for the families to claim at a later point, usually once the HAC has closed, through the family website.

The mortuary has several ways of identifying the deceased and is usually one that involves two scientific processes that are combined with the INTERPOL forms and approved by a panel of experts BEFORE a positive identification is given to the families. This can take time but requires the ultimate accuracy to ensure each identification is correct. Families can then make decisions around repatriation and other decisions about their loved ones before leaving the HAC (if they attended).

Personal effects is a service of returning items that belonged to the deceased to the families through a recorded and highly procedural process that ensures every single item found at the crash site is kept and archived so that families have the chance to claim what they believe may belong to their loved one.

Key Points from this Chapter

- Crash sites can be vast areas that require a scientific and methodical approach to referencing each item to ensure accuracy
- The mortuary has several key forensic areas that help with the identification process. Each is supported by an admin and records team
- The repatriation team needs to understand the whole journey to ensure export and import documents are accurate for all areas of the world and understand the size of the aircraft to allow for cargo or arrange other journey options, i.e., overground
- The personal effects teams are often not based at the crash site but in a facility that has the equipment, skills and infrastructure to hold, clean and repair personal effects to be catalogued
- Families can access the catalogues via the family website or via a hard copy

Quiz

1. Name the three scientific processes approved for a positive identification.
2. Name two of the teams that work within the mortuary to help with forensic identification.
3. Can a flag be placed on a coffin if being flown in an aircraft hold?
4. What are 'associated personal effects'? Give an example.
5. What are 'unassociated personal effects'? Give an example.
6. Name two items of personal effects that cannot legally be returned to families.
7. How many months is the best practice for storing personal effects?

Notes

1 Germanwings 4U9525 – A German low-cost carrier owned by Lufthansa and flying under the brand of Euroflyer. Crashed on 24 March 2015 in France, killing 144 on board. Flight routing was Barcelona – Düsseldorf.
2 Turkey and Syria earthquakes, February 2023. Magnitude of 7.8. Approx. 60K deaths.
3 MH370. Disappeared on 8 March 2014 having taken off from Kuala Lumpur en route to Beijing. 227 passengers and crew on board.
4 AF447. Crash mid-Atlantic 1 June 2009. Killed 228 on board. Took off from Rio de Janeiro enroute to Paris.

References and Additional Reading

College of Policing. (2019). *Practice Advice: The Medical Investigation of Suspected Homicide. Version 1.0.* (Online). Available at: www.college.police.uk/app/major-investigation-and-public-protection/homicide

ICAO. (2013). *Annex 9 to the Convention on International Civil Aviation Organization: 16th Ed. Facilitation.* Montreal: International Civil Aviation Organization.

ICAO. (2021). *Annex 13 to the Convention on International Civil Aviation Organization: 12th Ed. Aircraft Accident and Incident Investigation.* Montreal: International Civil Aviation Organization.

11 Closing an Operation

Chapter Objectives

By the end of this chapter, you will be able to:

- Explain how an aircraft accident response closes down
- Describe what a memorial event entails
- Understand why the one-year memorial is so important to families and survivors
- Explain how families and survivors are supported in the longer term

Glossary for this Chapter

CMC	Crisis Management Centre
IMC	Incident Management Centre
HAC	Humanitarian Assistance Centre
NGO	Non-Governmental Organisation
TEC	Telephone Enquiry Centre
TPP	Third Party Providers

Opening Quiz

1. Name some of the reasons that a HAC would close.
2. Why is the CMC involved at the end of an operation?
3. Why do we have a one-year memorial event?
4. Who should be invited to that event?
5. When does the operation transition to a 'longer-term support' phase?

Chapter Introduction

Every activation of a plan with the deployment of responders to a Humanitarian Assistance Centre (HAC) or even for a Telephone Enquiry Centre (TEC) must have a beginning and an end. It is as important to plan for the ending of an operation as it is to ensure the opening is as smooth as possible. The Crisis Management Centre (CMC) activation initiates the process of managing a response and supporting those involved, but that support must carry on right until the end of the operation and then beyond that.

DOI: 10.4324/9781003405337-14

In essence, the closing of an operation follows the reverse of the opening but with elements added for security, confidentiality and continuance. From the very first day of the HAC being open to welcome and support families of those who are injured or deceased, the management team and the insurers, authorities and investigation teams will be meeting to discuss the plan for how to and when to close the operation. Clearly, the preferred option would be to keep the HAC open until all those who are deceased have received a positive identification and the injured have gone home from hospital. This may not be realistic though, depending on the location of the accident, the size of the response and other factors such as geopolitics, conflict and security.

Working to a date in the future allows all parties to plan for resources and roster transfers. It allows for open communication with families so they can also plan and be prepared for the closing. Dates may have to change, but working to a planned date for closure is a more gentle and respectful gradual decrease in operations that does not leave the families feeling abandoned.

Once a date has been agreed in principle, then this should start to be communicated regularly to the families at the HAC. The reason for a regular '*countdown*' to closure is that families who are experiencing trauma cannot always listen and comprehend all that is being told to them. The art of being a good SAT member is to be able to know when to repeat important information gently. This means it may feel that the communication around closure is overdone. It is not.

Once a date has been discussed and agreed all parties should work to that in terms of gradually reducing the operation, personnel on site, room hire, etc. The management teams for the HAC will work closely at this point with the hotel management team, suppliers, Third Party Providers (TPP), agencies and anyone else involved to make sure the services, equipment and resources are still available but as families leave the HAC then the operation can contract accordingly.

Many families do not stay for long at the HAC. This is especially true if a positive identification of their loved one is going to be a long process or needs time to conclude through courts, etc. Families also have other family members at home who may need them, so often, families do leave the HAC before a positive identification. This is not unusual, but still, there will be families who cannot leave the HAC psychologically without the repatriation of their loved one once a positive identification has taken place. These families need extra support and communication as there will be a cut-off point when their expenses and accommodation etc., may not be covered by the insurance. The Special Assistance Team (SAT) and management team will work closely with these families to offer as much help and support as they possibly can so the support is still in place when they leave the HAC.

 Tip

I have deployed to several HACs where families simply refused to leave for a variety of reasons and paid to stay on themselves until such a point as they received their positive identification or realised they had to leave and go home. This is a challenging situation as they cannot be left unsupported, so consider having one or two SAT members remaining or using them in the country so families have a contact should they need immediate support or have questions.

Having fully communicated the closing date through the daily briefings where the families can ask questions about that process, additionally, through letters and emails (however they prefer) and by their SAT member sitting with them and explaining the process, the next phase is to start reducing personnel along with families leaving the HAC. This can be planned well in advance from the CMC, which, up to this point, has been supporting the Incident Management Centre (IMC) at the HAC.

At this point, the CMC would increase its personnel and take back some of the responsibilities that the IMC has undertaken at the HAC. That could be organising travel for SAT members and being a contact for the phone number for families. This allows the staff at the HAC to concentrate on reducing the operation and undertaking the essential elements to hand over information and data to the investigators and ensuring all parties involved understand their separate responsibilities once the HAC closes.

All notes, manuals and printed material should be handed over to the investigating authorities as evidence, and any information held on laptops should be stored securely and handed over as required. This is especially important if the laptops have been hired locally as they need to be returned clean and without any information being potentially visible.

As part of comprehensive plans for airlines at this point, there should be a relationship with a courier company that can air freight equipment from the mortuaries, HAC and IMC, etc., back to the airline base or Third Party Provider (TPP) facility if that is more appropriate. This can take a while to organise, so bringing them in at the point of deciding on the date for closing is essential.

Keeping a skeleton staff at the HAC even after closing for a few days would ensure that families who have decided to stay can have access to someone to ask about bills, accommodation and other logistical issues. Some airlines leave one or two people at the HAC as a daytime contact anyway, but this is something that, for each response, would need to be reviewed depending on numbers and profile, etc. The families would have the support number that would take them to the CMC for questions and would have all necessary contact details, usually through the family website and emails, as the HAC progresses from a live response to a post-response operation and longer-term support for those involved. Figure 11.1 shows how the reverse flow for closing a HAC takes place. It should mirror the opening in terms of phases.

If this is conducted well, the families, personnel and all involved can feel part of the process, feel supported and understand they still have access to information and airline personnel needed for their next phase of the grief journey. If, however, it is not undertaken well, families can feel abandoned and alone. This is where Family Associations play a vital role. They can advise on how they were treated, how they felt and what worked for them so airlines can make sure they really work to continue the support needed as opposed to '*walking away*'.

Post Response Phase

For each crisis, it will be different, and it will depend on the severity of the accident, how many people were involved, the mix of survivors and families of deceased, the culture and religions involved and region of the world in which it took place.

The Family Assistance Act (1996/2000) and ICAO Documents 9993 and 9997 all provide for families and survivors, stating that support should continue afterwards, but the questions that remain unanswered in all of this are '*How long and in what format?*'

'*How long?*' is difficult, but airlines can support families for years if they choose to. It could be that because of the nature of the accident, the families need extra support, communication, access to information, etc., for many years. An example of this is MH370, where families of those who were onboard remain in communication with the airline, investigation teams, etc. This is an extreme example, but usually a year is not unusual (see Chapter 9).

Support could be through a variety of channels: through the family website, where they can contact someone via email, which is becoming increasingly more popular as a choice for

Figure 11.1 Reverse flow for closing the HAC

continued support, or via a dedicated phone line (toll-free) that is monitored and handled by a trained team who know and understand the family's needs. It could be that initially, after the HAC closes, the website and phone numbers are monitored 24/7 and then gradually reduced as time goes on, perhaps increasing again temporarily towards the memorial at one year and then moving to a more regular monitoring plan after that. All these options are relevant depending on the accident itself and probably cannot be decided until the time.

In Chapter 8, the family website was explored. This is something that, once the accident response has ceased to be a '*live*' event, can really help to inform and support families and survivors for as long as is necessary, as long as it remains updated and monitored.

Each family gets a unique login and can access documents from the authorities and investigators, media statements from the airline or authorities as they are released and contact for support and queries. It also helps to prepare the families and survivors for the one-year memorial, so it is a vital component that needs to be planned for and utilised appropriately.

 Observation

Up to ten years ago, all contact with families and survivors was face-to-face. Then the family websites began to appear, and I was surprised how quickly families and survivors adopted this as the '*go-to*' point for information and communication. It coincided with a decrease in families coming to the HAC. There is definitely an evolution towards more support given while families stay at home rather than them coming to a physical building. I found this increased during the pandemic when I was activated to an incident through a TPP but attended remotely to a virtual HAC. Technology and changes in how society communicates, etc., means the family website is becoming an increasingly important part of the plans, not a '*nice-to-have*' add-on.

Memorials

A memorial can take several forms. As discussed in Chapter 7, the first is often five to six days into the HAC opening, held at the HAC or a nearby venue for families, those involved in the operation, authorities and investigators, etc., as a small, usually non-denominational memorial organised by the HAC management team and SATs.

The other is a formal, more high-profile event marking the one-year anniversary of the accident. This section will concentrate on this as it forms part of the planning process, can be extremely challenging to organise and run and has a media presence.

Organisation for the one-year memorial should start quite early on. Clearly, the emphasis and concentration of everyone at the airline and TPP, etc., is supporting the families of the deceased, obtaining positive identifications, repatriation, personal effects, etc., and supporting survivors, but in the background, there should be some early planning of the memorial. Leaving it until nearer the time can cause lots of challenges that could be avoided if tackled much earlier.

Although not specifically stipulated, having a team dedicated to the memorial and away from the accident response can be beneficial as it allows for a focused approach to what can be a large and high-profile event. Towards the memorial itself, having members of the SAT team join the memorial team can also support extra understanding of the families, the experience at the HAC and a more sensitive and compassionate approach.

What is stipulated in the Family Assistance Act (1996/2000) is that the families and survivors must be involved in the memorial service, the final design of the memorial *'stone'* (if applicable) and any other elements of the memorial that could require a decision on direction, design and implementation. This can be challenging for the organisers, given the event itself and the fact it is less than a year since the accident.

Open and detailed communication is key, but also understanding some families and survivors may not want, or feel able, to be part of the decision-making process for a variety of reasons. As long as they have the opportunity to offer their thoughts and ideas, then this does cover the requirements of the Act.

The first and probably the most important part of the memorial is understanding what the memorial itself will look like and where it should be positioned. Some of the key issues could be if the accident occurred in the sea or a geopolitical region, deciding where the most appropriate place to locate it is important, as is deciding whether to have one at the departure location, the arrival location, or both. The other point to consider would be depending on where it is, it should be accessible for families, friends, survivors, and the public to view, and this might restrict the location, e.g., not airside at an airport or an area with restricted access. These decisions can be challenging for everyone concerned (Greenwald, 2010).

What the memorial looks like is also a delicate matter as they can vary so much from accident to accident. The Act does not stipulate how to manage this, but often, having a choice of two or three for families to choose from can be the most useful process. Rendering the design of the memorial and then offering the families and survivors a vote either via letter or via the family website can reduce disputes or discordance.

The wording on the memorials can also be decided in a similar process, and a good example of this is the memorial stone for EgyptAir 804 in May 2016.[1] It was made of marble and engraved with a passage in French, Arabic and English. The families were able to decide what to include, what order to put the passages in and the size, shape and positioning of the memorial. As this shows, this is not something that can be organised with a month to go.

 Observation

As part of the organising team for a memorial event, many families refused to take part in the decision-making process, attend the ceremony and have their loved one's names included at the memorial site itself. To future-proof this, enough blank plaques were set aside at the site itself to allow for families to change their minds without causing too much disturbance to the memorial.

Media at the Memorials

All one-year memorials are high profile, and the organising team needs to understand that the memorial event is a media opportunity. This is especially true if the final report has been published, is controversial or there are political elements included in it. It is not possible to exclude media from the memorials, so managing their presence and establishing a protocol for behaviour, taking photos, interviewing families and survivors, etc., needs to be established early on and agreed to.

Having a suitable building for the memorial ceremony itself may need some considerable thought. The obvious choice to ensure enough space might be a religious building, but it may not be appropriate for families who do not share the religion. It may be more diplomatic to have a temporary structure depending on location and weather conditions, i.e., extreme heat. This can also have the effect of feeling *'clinical'* or *'cold'*, so having the families' and survivors' agreement is essential without imposing the structure on them.

Once the structure has been agreed and the design for the memorial rendered, the next element to consider is the ceremony itself and who to invite. There are no set rules for this, except the most important groups are the families and the survivors. They must take precedence over representatives from the airline, authorities involved, ambassadors, investigating teams, TPP, airport, search and rescue/recovery, family organisations, NGOs and any other groups that were part of the operation. As you can see, this can start to build up to an enormous number of guests.

Some families and survivors may not wish to travel or attend, just as they may have attended the HAC. Access to the ceremony via *'livestream'* through the family website is essential and can support any restriction on numbers. However, depending on where the ceremony is held, there can be a restriction on *'band width'*, which can restrict the quality of the *'livestream'* event.

For most memorials where families, friends and survivors might need to travel, it is prudent to re-open the HAC for a short period of time. The organising team will know, in advance potentially, how many people may need to travel to the memorial, given how many travelled to the HAC. Although not an exact science, it can help for planning purposes. Using the SAT team that managed and worked at the HAC initially means they are familiar with what needs to be in place and can easily and quickly open the HAC.

How the HAC works for a memorial is, of course, slightly different from the initial operation. The difference is that the HAC will be open from a set date in the future, operated for the sole use of logistical and accommodation support for those visiting for the memorial event, and a family briefing from the airline, authorities, etc., whilst there especially if the report has been released, or is due for release.

The setup could mirror the HAC for the initial operation, an operational office but not necessarily an IMC. There needs to be accommodation for those who may visit, the SAT members and officials if using the HAC and HAC services, i.e., food and beverages. This can be organised by a subset of the memorial team made up of SAT members and the personnel familiar with the HAC used and who know what is needed and can ensure everything is ready.

Printed materials in several languages will be required at the memorial event. The agenda for the memorial and any briefings at the HAC alongside the *'programme for the event'*. Transport will need to be organised so there are enough resources available to safely move the families to and from the HAC to the event and back again, alongside any security that might be required. This can be organised in advance and have the personnel in place in plenty of time for the first families to arrive.

Not all families and survivors might wish to return to the HAC for a variety of reasons. In many cases, they stay where they are and use the *'livestream'* facilities to view the memorial itself. This might also need to be planned to ensure any technical resources that need to be set up for the families can be undertaken in plenty of time, and they may also require SAT members to be sent to their houses to support set up and emotional support for the event itself. Communicating with the families well in advance is key to understanding the size of the HAC, the size and scope of the memorial, how many SAT members will be needed, and the technical teams required.

The families really are the decision makers throughout this process for the memorial. Frequent communication is key to keeping them updated on any decisions made, the progress of the organising and ensuring their feelings, thoughts and ideas are considered. Not all families want to take part, and some families want to take part in all of the decisions, but the balance here is about being honest, open and truthful about what can be achieved and what cannot, given any restrictions being put in place, i.e., numbers at the event, the size of memorial and programme of the event itself.

Re-Opening the Humanitarian Assistance Centre

Once a date for opening the HAC has been decided, sending a team to be based there for the month beforehand is recommended to make sure they are on-site for any decisions to be made and to problem-solve in plenty of time. This works well to minimise mistakes and challenges. This allows for practice runs for transporting large numbers of people to and from the event location, timings for the programme itself, practicing the event, etc.

Any printing and language translation for the programme, etc., can be undertaken at the HAC to minimise transportation costs. Also, the team can help to set up the memorial event and have things almost ready for when the main team arrives.

Often, these events include a *'memorial gift'* as part of the service. It could be a piece of marble from the main memorial stone or a flower and candle, for example, along with a programme for the service. Depending on who is coming to the event, this may need to be organised in plenty of time, and the organising team at the site can help to arrange this locally.

When families start to arrive for the memorial event, the same process as before should be initiated. Collection from the airport by a SAT member, transported to the HAC, badging, a meeting to explain how the HAC will work and the transport arrangements for the event itself. Let them know when there will be a briefing held and how to get hold of the team in the office whilst there.

On the day itself, having lots of teams available to help with transport and seating in plenty of time for any security arrangements is essential.

One of the key issues is where to seat everyone. Understandably, there will be celebrities or dignitaries attending, and the urge is sometimes to sit them at the front, but it is vital that the families, friends and survivors remain the key focus of the event. Seat them at the front nearest the stage (if you have a stage), and the dignitaries should be seated behind them. This can mitigate any potential for feeling left out and *'second best'* from the families. It is a simple mistake to make, but it can cause such bad feelings to undo any of the good built up over the year through support.

Often, the memorial event will be attended by ambassadors and government representatives, investigators and many of the initial responding teams. Airlines need to arrange this and be in contact with the various parties to understand who is coming and who might not attend.

Understanding where to place media and making the families aware that there will be a media presence and if they want to interact with the media, how to do this so as not to interfere with other families can be explained well in advance.

The event itself can be as unique as each accident is. Decisions include if there will be speakers and who these might be, if there will be singing, whether the event will be multiple denominational or non-denominational, what flowers will be offered, whether the families be able to go up to and touch the memorial itself at the event and what time of day to hold the event and whether it should coincide with the crash timing or not. These are all key elements of the memorial.

Closing the Humanitarian Assistance Centre after the Memorial

Often, the HAC will close the day after the memorial event or two days after if there are to be private visits to the memorial by the families. The closing should be fairly quick and simple, given it is not to the same scale or size as the initial accident response. The most the HAC should be open is for one week to consider receiving those coming to the event and saying goodbye to them.

Examples of the Variety of Memorials

As discussed earlier in this chapter, the range of the memorials used is varied, and the families and survivors are part of the decision-making for the final design. This section includes a small selection of examples to illustrate this. Figures 11.2, 11.3, and 11.4 are memorials that show the sheer variety and range of memorials in different locations around the world.

Often, the memorial itself has letters or items from the families included. It may also have unidentified human remains, as discussed in Chapter 10.

Figure 11.2 National memorial for victims of 9/11

Figure 11.3 Memorial for Northwest Orient Airlines Flight 710

Attribution: Dcmcgov, Public domain, via Wikimedia Commons

Figure 11.4 Memorial with panoramic surround for Flash Airlines 604

Attribution: Doomych, Public domain, via Wikimedia Commons

Conclusions

How to close a HAC and transition to a longer-term support approach is as important as opening one. Communication with the families and survivors needs to be constant, open and truthful. Offering post-operation support through whatever channel works best for the situation can alleviate some of the worry around feeling *'abandoned'*, and also using Family Associations to advise and guide the airline can help with making this as gentle and compassionate as possible.

The memorial needs to be organised well in advance as they tend to be high-profile media events. Families need to be included in the design of the memorial, where it is located (as much as possible) and the programme of the event itself. Again, communication needs to come from the airline and be as open and honest as possible. Not everyone wants to be involved in the decision-making or even attend the memorial, and as long as they have been given the opportunity to do so, it is entirely their choice. Some families may choose to watch the event through the family website if it is *'livestreamed'*.

The event can include those involved in the post-accident operation, dignitaries, celebrities, government officials and ambassadors, but the focus must always be the families and survivors in all areas of the organisation of the memorial event.

The location and design of the memorial is as unique as the event itself and should always reflect the families' and survivors' wishes.

Key Points from this Chapter

- The closing of the HAC needs to be planned from the day the HAC opens, and families and survivors must be kept informed regularly
- Not all families will leave the HAC with a positive identification or with their loved one. This can be challenging to manage and support
- The transition to close the HAC can be gradual to reduce resources and equipment, etc., whilst still offering all the required services to the families
- Not all families leave the HAC when it closes. Some choose to stay and pay for themselves, and in this case, the airline should consider leaving a small team of SAT members at the HAC as a contact
- The memorial is a high-profile media event and needs to be organised down to the tiniest detail
- The HAC may well need to be opened again for a short period of time with reduced services for the few days around the memorial event
- Not all families and survivors will want to come to the event. Some may want nothing to do with the decision-making process, but others will want to be fully *'immersed'* and both these decisions should be supported by the airline

Quiz

Take a few minutes to complete this quiz to check your understanding of this chapter.

1. Why is it important to hand over all notes, manuals and data from laptops to the investigation authorities?
2. Why do you need to keep communicating the closing date to families whilst they are at the HAC?

3. What decisions can families and survivors make around the memorial event?
4. Where would you seat the families and survivors at the memorial event?
5. Why does the HAC re-open for the memorial event, and for how long approximately?
6. Who can you expect to attend the memorial event apart from the families and survivors?
7. If families cannot attend the event or choose not to, how might they be able to watch it?

Note

1 EgyptAir 804. Crashed 19 May 2016, killing 66 on board. Took off from Paris en route to Cairo.

References and Additional Reading

Family Assistance Act. (1996/2000). (Online). Available at: www.ntsb.gov/tda/er/Pages/tda-fa-aviation.aspx.
Greenwald, A. (2010). "Passion on All Sides": Lessons for Planning the National September 11 Memorial Museum. *Curator*, 53 (1) pp. 117–125. https://doi.org/10.1111/j.2151–6952.2009.00012.x.

Index

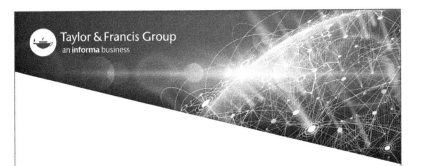

For Product Safety Concerns and Information please contact our EU
representative GPSR@taylorandfrancis.com
Taylor & Francis Verlag GmbH, Kaufingerstraße 24, 80331 München, Germany

www.ingramcontent.com/pod-product-compliance
Ingram Content Group UK Ltd.
Pitfield, Milton Keynes, MK11 3LW, UK
UKHW011456240425
457818UK00022B/868